D1595628

Unless Recalled Earlier

OCEANIAN HISTORICAL DICTIONARIES

Edited by Jon Woronoff

HISTORICAL DICTIONARY OF GUAM AND MICRONESIA

by
William L. Wuerch and
Dirk Anthony Ballendorf

Oceanian Historical Dictionaries, No. 3

The Scarecrow Press, Inc.
Lanham, Md., & London

British Library Cataloguing-in-Publication data available

Library of Congress Cataloging-in-Publication Data

Wuerch, William L.
    Historical dictionary of Guam and Micronesia / by William L. Wuerch and
Dirk Anthony Ballendorf.
       p.   cm. — (Oceanian historical dictionaries ; no. 3)
    Includes bibliographical references.
    ISBN 0-8108-2858-8 (acid-free paper)
    1. Micronesia—History—Dictionaries. 2. Guam—History—Dictionar-
ies. I. Ballendorf, Dirk Anthony, 1939– . II. Title. III. Series.
DU500.W84   1994
996.5′003—dc20   94-5672

TO APPLE AND PACA

CONTENTS

EDITOR'S FOREWORD

Micronesia, although located on the other side of the Pacific, is of particular interest to the United States. For, among its seven political entities, three are countries ''freely associated'' with the United States and two are U.S. territories. The remaining two are independent countries, a status that should become more widespread with time. For that reason, among many others, Micronesia should also interest other nations, including neighbors like Australia and a more distant Japan and those in the Pacific Basin in general. Such interest can take many forms, investment, trade, tourism, and so on. But it should certainly include the intriguing histories and cultures of the region as well as their political institutions and economic potential.

While there is some interest in Micronesia already, there should be much more over the coming years. The problem is thus, for those who want to know more, where to seek information about the region. Not enough has been written about Micronesia as a whole or its component parts, and what does exist is not always readily accessible or carefully organized. This *Historical Dictionary of Guam and Micronesia* therefore fills a big gap. It offers a look backward at the past, a look around at the present, and even the basis for a look into the future in an extensive chronology, a solid introduction, and numerous specific entries on persons, places, institutions, events, and so on. It concludes with a very comprehensive bibliography.

This volume was written by two men who know Micronesia thoroughly, having lived and taught there for many years. William L. Wuerch is manuscripts librarian at the University of Guam's Micronesian Area Research Center. In addition to several bibliographies, he has written many articles and monographs on Micronesian history. Dirk Anthony Ballendorf is professor of Micronesian studies at the University of Guam's Micronesian Area Research Center and was the center's director for five years. He, too, has written extensively on Micronesia and edited *Glimpses Magazine*. Their knowledge and experience combined to produce an extremely useful guide to a part of the world that deserves to be better known.

Jon Woronoff
Series Editor

INTRODUCTION

Micronesia is a collection of island groups in the northwest Pacific Ocean comprised of five major clusters: the Marianas, Carolines, Marshalls, the Gilbert Islands, and Nauru. Their general location is from five degrees, twenty minutes north latitude, and from 130 to 180 degrees east longitude. Their total land and sea area is approximately the size of the United States, although the total land area would come to about one half of the state of Rhode Island or approximately the same size as the European Principality of Liechtenstein. If Micronesia were superimposed on a map of Europe and Asia, it would stretch from London to Tehran.

There are several definitions of the term Micronesia. Geographically, Micronesia includes the Marianas, the Carolines, the Marshalls, the Gilbert Islands, and Nauru. Culturally, Micronesia includes generally the same groups, although there is a heavy Polynesian influence at Kapingamarangi Atoll, which is near the equator south of Chuuk (Truk) and Pohnpei, and a Melanesian influence at Tobi Island in Palau. Some ethnographers have considered Tuvalu (formerly the Ellice Islands) to be culturally Micronesian. Altogether, linguistically, ten distinct language groups have been identified in Micronesia.

The political definition of Micronesia, however, is somewhat narrower. Since the end of the second World War, Micronesia has been regarded as being synonymous with the Trust Territory of the Pacific Islands (TTPI), which included only the Marianas (except Guam), the Carolines, and the Marshalls. The Gilberts became part of the independent nation of Kiribati in 1979, while Nauru, another trust territory and an island rich in phosphate reserves, is also independent. In 1975 for the Marianas, and in 1978 for the other areas, the people of Micronesia decided on a political status of free association and commonwealth with the United States and divided themselves into four distinct political entities: (1) the Republic of the Marshall Islands, (2) the Republic of Palau, (3) the Federated States of Micronesia, and (4) the

Commonwealth of the Northern Mariana Islands. Following plebiscites in 1979 on their constitutions, all of the entities except Palau became autonomous in 1986. Palau remains the single entity comprising the TTPI pending the electoral ratification of their Compact of Free Association with the United States, or deciding upon some other status, that is, independence.

There are a number of different designations and spellings now for the new Micronesian states, and these have come about as the result of the growing nationalism from changing political status from trusteeship to autonomy. Some examples are Ponape, which has now become Pohnpei after the local pronunciation and spelling. In the local language Pohnpei translates as ''upon a stone altar.'' Truk, long the name and spelling used by colonials, has become Chuuk after the local form. Palau is Belau in the local language; Palauans, however, make the point that Belau is to be used only when speaking the local language. Hence the colonial version remains in common use even within Palau.

The early Micronesians began their migrations to the region from southeast Asia about 10,000 years ago; the region was the last major area of the world to be peopled in various migratory phases from both the east and west. Ferdinand Magellan was the first European known to have landed in the region; he touched briefly at Guam in March 1521 during his famous circumnavigation of the world. His voyage established the Spanish claim to the islands, although it was not until 1668 that the Spanish actually began a permanent colony, and then primarily at Guam. Spain's primary interest was in converting natives to Christianity in the form of baptized Catholics. The Marianas natives, called Chamorros, rebelled against the Spanish but were subdued in a series of bloody conflicts known as the ''Chamorro wars'' and by 1695 were subjugated under the authority of the Spanish crown. For the next two centuries Spain ruled the Marianas as a colony, which was an important stop on the Manila galleon route until 1815, and thereafter a backwater visited occasionally by traders and whalers.

In the nineteenth century, whaling was an important industry in Micronesia and elsewhere in the Pacific. Whales were sought for oil that was produced from their heads and thick skin, called blubber. The head of a large sperm whale could contain as much as 5,000 gallons of sperm oil, which in 1866, the peak price year, sold for $2.55 per gallon. Oil from the blubber sold for $1.45 per gallon, and even whalebone brought profits of $1.25 per pound. In 1840 a million gallons of whale oil and two million pounds of bone were exported to the United States, much of it coming from Micronesia.

Spain remained in control of most of Micronesia until the Spanish-American War of 1898. Following that conflict, Germany purchased all of Micronesia, except Guam, which the Americans retained, and the Gilberts, which had been made a British protectorate in 1892. The Germans were interested in economic development and invested in agriculture with a view of developing the production of copra—the dried meat of coconuts from which an exquisite and versatile oil is refined. Known then as "Micronesian gold," it brought high prices on the world market of that day. The Germans were plagued by typhoons and insect pests, however, and their investments failed to bring in the projected profits. The German administration also had difficulty enticing colonists from the fatherland to settle in the islands.

In 1914, with the outbreak of World War I, Japan seized Micronesia from the Germans in a calculated strategic move. Australia seized German Nauru in 1914. During three weeks in October of that year, the Japanese Imperial navy occupied all the centers in the Marshalls, Marianas, and Carolines under the terms of secret agreements they had made with the British. After WWI, and upon the insistence of the United States, Japan applied for membership in the League of Nations and arranged to govern her Micronesian islands as a mandate. This agreement was formalized and took effect officially in 1922. The Japanese efforts at economic development were tremendous, far greater than anything the Germans had attempted before them. Besides agriculture, mining, fishing, and food processing, the Japanese promoted economic development and brought thousands of Japanese settlers from the home islands and their other colonies during the 1920s and 1930s. After WWI Nauru was also placed under a League of Nations mandate to be jointly administered by the United Kingdom, New Zealand, and Australia. The Gilberts had been annexed by the United Kingdom during the war.

By the mid-1930s, sugar cultivation and refining alone accounted for some 66 percent of the total revenues in Micronesia. This industry was centered in the Marianas, especially the islands of Saipan, Tinian, and Rota. Phosphate was mined at Anguar in

Palau and at Rota in the Marianas, and workers were imported from other Micronesian islands, as well as from Taiwan, Korea, and other parts of the growing Japanese empire. After 1935 when Japan withdrew from the League of Nations, the islands came increasingly under the influence of the Japanese military authority and were gradually and systematically girded for war with the West.

Guam had been administered by a U.S. naval government from 1898 until the outbreak of WWII when it was invaded and occupied by Japanese Imperial forces from 10 December 1941 until 21 July 1944, when American forces recaptured the island. The Japanese also occupied the Gilberts and Nauru during WWII.

In a series of bloody battles, the Americans wrested the islands from the Japanese over a two-and-a-half-year period from early 1942 to late 1944. The American war machine destroyed the Japanese infrasctructure. Following the end of the war, all Japanese nationals were repatriated to their home islands, which not only reduced the population by some 77,000, but also caused the Micronesian economy to collapse. Into this vacuum came American naval officials under the authority of the United Nations Trusteeship Agreement and then began the task of rebuilding and developing the Micronesian social and economic, as well as political capacities, almost completely from scratch.

The United States has administered Micronesia under this agreement ever since, although since 1979 when the new constitutions were ratified, the American administration treated the island groups as virtually autonomous even though the trusteeship agreement was still technically in effect.

Negotiations toward a post-trusteeship political status began between the Micronesians and Americans in 1968. At that time the TTPI was divided into six administrative districts: Marianas, Yap, Palau, Truk, Ponape, and the Marshalls. The seventh district of Kosrae was divided from the Ponape district in 1975. But, as the future political status negotiations progressed slowly over the years, it became clear that these districts wished to align themselves differently. During President Gerald Ford's administration, a status of free association with the United States was finally decided upon. This status would be finalized by a document called a Compact, which is akin to a treaty describing the relationship. Subsequently, under this arrangement, the seven districts of the

TTPI divided themselves into three new national "freely associated states," and one separate commonwealth of the United States, making a total of four separate political entities. These are: (1) the Republic of Palau, formerly the Palau district and still a trust territory; (2) the Federated States of Micronesia (FSM), formerly the districts of Yap, Truk, Ponape, and Kosrae; (3) the Republic of the Marshall Islands; and, (4) the Commonwealth of the Northern Mariana Islands (CNMI), formerly the Marianas district.

In 1986 the United States unilaterally lifted application of the trusteeship in the cases of the FSM, the Marshalls, and the CNMI. Palau remained under the trusteeship agreement. Its constitution was in conflict with its negotiated Compact of Free Association and the people failed to ratify the terms of the Compact until now. Guam is a part of Micronesia as well, but it has been politically separate since the end of the Spanish times in 1898; Guam is an unincorporated American territory.

During the American times in Micronesia, social, political, and economic progress has not been as vigorous or as rapid as both Micronesians and Americans would have liked. During the first twenty years of the American trusteeship, the annual budgets for the territory never exceeded $8 million. During President John F. Kennedy's administration, the ceiling levels were doubled, and a number of federal programs—normally designed and reserved for the fifty states—were extended to the Trust Territory. These programs were further increased during the administration of Lyndon Johnson under the Great Society Program. The United States Peace Corps began to make a variety of volunteer assignments in Micronesia in 1966, and by 1968 there were more than 800 Peace Corps volunteers and trainees serving in the islands. Although these numbers were considerably reduced by the mid-1970s, the level of spoken English throughout Micronesia rose markedly, as did political awareness, as a result of the Peace Corps' efforts.

American programs in social development resulted in many young Micronesians going abroad to participate in higher education programs, especially in the United States. Public health facilities were also improved with three large new hospitals constructed and in operation by 1980. The testing of thermonuclear devices in the Marshall Islands in the 1940s and 1950s caused several hundred islanders to be displaced from their homes, and the United States government through a variety of legal arrangements, compensated and relocated these families and has also provided for an extended and generous trust fund to be established for their posterity.

Although there are no military bases per se in Micronesia, there are military personnel assigned to various islands as part of 13-man construction crews to improve and build various minor public works installations such as docks, roads, bridges, and recreational facilities. These military Civil Action Teams (CAT) also train locals in construction vocational skills. Harbor facilities and airplane runways have been enlarged or constructed at the major airports and also at some of the more remote locations.

The final termination date of the trusteeship for Palau has not been set yet. The Compact still awaits approval in a plebiscite. In the meantime the trusteeship remains in effect for Palau. In 1991 the Federated States of Micronesia and the Marshall Islands Republic became full members of the United Nations.

Guam remains an unincorporated territory of the United States, although there has been submitted to the U.S. Congress a draft act for commonwealth status, and negotiations toward this status continue. Nauru, rich in phosphate, became a United Nations trusteeship under Australia in 1947, and full independence was granted in 1968. The Gilberts were under British administration until 1979 when they became part of the independent nation of Kiribati.

Currently, there are thirty-four independent, autonomous, and territorial political entities in the wider Pacific, with seven being in the Micronesian region.

William L. Wuerch
Dirk Anthony Ballendorf
1994

HISTORICAL CHRONOLOGY
OF GUAM AND MICRONESIA

7,000,000 B.C.	Mariana Islands formed by volcanos.
12,000 B.C.	Micronesia and the Pacific peopled.
2,000 B.C.	First people arrive in the Marianas.
2,000 to 500 B.C.	The greatest period of migrations into Micronesia and the wider Pacific.
1,500 B.C.	Saipan peopled.
1,000 B.C.	Palau and Yap peopled.
A.D. 800	Latte stone culture appears in the Marianas.
1521	Magellan reaches Guam.
1525	Rocha at Yap.
1528	Saavedra discovers Marshalls.
1565	Legaspi's voyage to the Philippines. Guam Galleon trade begins.
1568	Mendana in Marshalls.
1579	Drake at Palau.
1595	Quiros sights Pohnpei.
1602	Fray Juan Pobre living among the Chamorros.

1606	Quiros sights Gilbert Islands.
1662	Sanvitores first visits Marianas.
1668	Sanvitores founds Marianas mission on Guam.
1669	First church and school built on Guam.
1670	Spanish-Chamorro wars begin on Guam.
1672	Sanvitores killed by Chamorros.
1683	Esplana and Quiroga arrive on Guam.
1686	Dampier at Guam. Caroline Islands named the New Philippines by Spain.
1695	Chamorros subdued.
1700	Epidemics in Marianas. Northern islanders brought to Guam.
1742	Anson and *Centurion* at Tinian.
1771	Governor Tobias arrives in Marianas.
1783	*Antelope* wrecked at Palau; Lee Boo taken to London.
1787	Lamotrek canoes begin visits to Guam.
1788	Gilbert and Marshall in Micronesia.
1801	*Lydia* first American ship to visit Guam.
1815	End of galleon trade.
1817	Kotzebue in Marshalls.

| 1818 | Carolinians begin to settle on Saipan. |

| 1819 | Freycinet at Guam. |

| 1824 | Duperrey's expedition at Kosrae. Kotzebue's second expedition to Marshalls. *Globe* mutiny. |

| 1828 | Lutke mapping Carolines. Dumont D'Urville's first voyage. Villalobos investigation of Guam. |

| 1830 | J. F. O'Connell on Pohnpei. |

| 1837 | Ngatik massacre. |

| 1838 | Dumont D'Urville's second expedition. |

| 1840 | American whaleships begin to visit in large numbers. |

| 1841 | Wilkes expedition in Micronesia. |

| 1843 | Cheyne begins trade on Pohnpei. |

| 1852 | Missions set up on Pohnpei and Kosrae. |

| 1854 | Smallpox epidemic on Pohnpei. U.S. consul Samuel Masters stationed at Guam. |

| 1855 | Annual allowance for Marianas ends. Peak whaling year at Pohnpei and Kosrae. Godeffroy agents visit Carolines. |

| 1856 | Smallpox epidemic on Guam. |

| 1857 | First Protestant missions in the Marshalls and Gilberts. *Morning Star* on first Micronesian cruise. |

| 1860 | Capelle starts copra trade in Marshalls. |

1862	Semper conducting fieldwork in Palau.
1865	*Shenandoah* at Pohnpei.
1866	Pease begins operations on Pohnpei.
1869	Godeffroy station opens on Yap.
1871	Kubary begins Palauan studies.
1871	Bully Hayes arrives in Micronesia.
1872	First blackbirders call in Micronesia. O'Keefe begins trade on Yap.
1873	Holcomb arrives on Yap.
1875	All Kosraeans become church members.
1877	Bully Hayes killed in the Marshalls.
1879	Protestant missions started in Truk lagoon. Deutschehandels und Plantengen Gesellschaft takes over Godeffroy trade.
1885	Coaling station set up on Yap. Germany and Spain contest Carolines; Germany annexes Marshalls.
1886	Spanish governor installed on Yap.
1887	Spanish governor installed on Pohnpei. First Pohnpeian uprising; Spanish governor killed.
1888	Nauru incorporated in the German Marshall Islands Protectorate.
1890	Second Pohnpeian uprising.
1892	British protectorate over Gilberts.

1898   Spanish-American War; U.S. captures Guam.

1899   Germany purchases Carolines and Marianas;
            United States occupies Guam; first naval gov-
            ernor arrives. Protestant missionaries arrive on
            Nauru.

1901   Protestant missionaries arrive on Guam.

1903   Catholic missionaries arrive on Nauru.

1909   Phosphate mining begins on Anguar. German
            South Seas Expedition in Micronesia.

1910   Sokehs Rebellion.

1914   Japan annexes German islands. Australia takes
            possession of Nauru.

1915   Great Britain annexes Gilbert and Ellice islands.
            Bank of Guam established.

1917   *Cormoran* scuttled at Guam. First Guam Con-
            gress appointed. Guam flag first flown.

1919   League of Nations granted Nauru as joint man-
            date to Australia, New Zealand, and Great Brit-
            ain.

1921   Japan given Micronesian mandate by League of
            Nations.

1922   Civil government in Japanese mandates. Wash-
            ington Naval Conference held.

1923   Guam's first golf course established.

1931   Guam Congress elected for first time. Women
            on Guam enfranchised.

1935   *China Clipper* begins service.

1936	Guamanians petition U.S. Congress for citizenship and civil rights; they are unsuccessful.
1941	Japan attacks Pearl Harbor and Guam.
1942	Japan occupies Nauru.
1942–1944	U.S. forces conquer Japanese islands, liberate Guam.
1945	U.S. Naval policy for islands issued. Naval Administration on Guam re-established. Australian troops reoccupy Nauru.
1946	Atomic tests begin on Bikini.
1947	Trust Territory of the Pacific Islands established, to be administered by U.S. Nauru becomes a United Nations Trust Territory administered by Australia.
1948	Atomic tests begin on Eniwetak.
1949	First civilian governor of Guam appointed. War crimes trials in Micronesia conclude.
1950	Organic Act for Guam signed by President Harry S Truman.
1951	Missile-testing facility set up on Kwajelein.
1952	College of Guam established.
1958	Nuclear testing in the Marshalls ends.
1960	First Chamorro appointed governor of Guam.
1962	U.S. Navy security clearance for Guam lifted. Solomon mission to Trust Territory.

1965	First Guam Washington Representative elected. Congress of Micronesia created.
1966	Peace Corps volunteers arrive in Micronesia.
1968	Nauru gains independence from Australia.
1970	First elected governor of Guam. Community College of Micronesia established.
1972	First Guam member of U.S. Congress installed. WWII Japanese soldier discovered on Guam.
1976	Guam plebiscite on political status.
1977	College of Micronesia established at Pohnpei. Guam Constitutional Convention.
1978	Commonwealth government installed in the Northern Marianas. Constitution of Federated States of Micronesia ratified.
1979	Gilberts become part of Republic of Kiribati. Guam's draft constitution rejected by voters.
1981	Pope John Paul II visits Guam.
1982	Guam plebiscite on political status: Commonwealth most popular. Compact of Free Association signed between Federated States of Micronesia and United States.
1984	First archbishop of Agana appointed.
1985	San Vitores beatified in Rome.
1986	U.N. Trusteeship in Northern Marianas terminated, Commonwealth Covenant in full effect. U.N. Trusteeship ends for Marshalls, Eastern Carolines.

1988   Guam's Commonwealth Draft Act introduced in U.S. Congress.

1990   USSR recognizes end of Trusteeship for Federated States of Micronesia and the Republic of the Marshall Islands.

1991   Full U.N. membership for Federated States of Micronesia and the Republic of the Marshall Islands. Palauans reject Compact for tenth time.

ABBREVIATIONS AND ACRONYMS

ABCFM	American Board of Commissioners for Foreign Missions.
AK	Atkins-Kroll
CAT	Civil Action Team
CCM	Community College of Micronesia
CIA	Central Intelligence Agency
CIMA	Coordinated Investigation of Micronesian Anthropology
CinCPAC	Commander in Chief, Pacific Area Command
CNMI	Commonwealth of the Northern Mariana Islands
COMNAVMAR	Commander, Naval Forces, Marianas
DOE	Department of Education
FSM	Federated States of Micronesia
MARC	Micronesian Area Research Center
MOC	Micronesian Occupational College
MTEC	Micronesian Teacher Education Center
NBK	Nan'yo Boeki Kaisha

NTTU	Naval Technical Training Units
OEK	Olbiil Era Kelulau
PBMOTP	Pacific Basin Medical Officers Training Program
PITTS	Pacific Islands Teachers Training School
RMI	Republic of the Marshall Islands
ROP	Republic of Palau
TTPI	Trust Territory of the Pacific Islands
U.N.	United Nations
UOG	University of Guam
U.S.	United States
USCC	United States Commercial Company
USMC	United States Marine Corps
USN	United States Navy
USSR	Union of Soviet Socialist Republics
WWI	World War One
WWII	World War Two

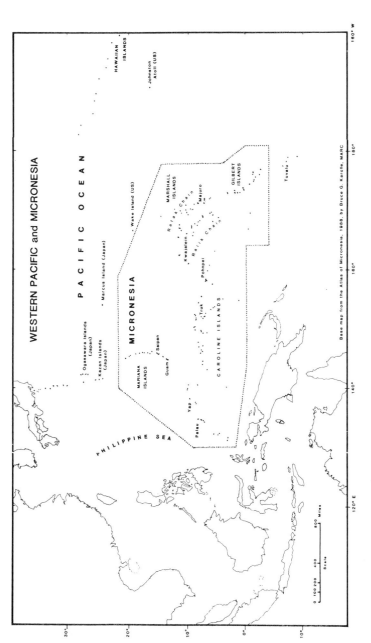

The Western Pacific and Micronesia (copyright B. Karolle)

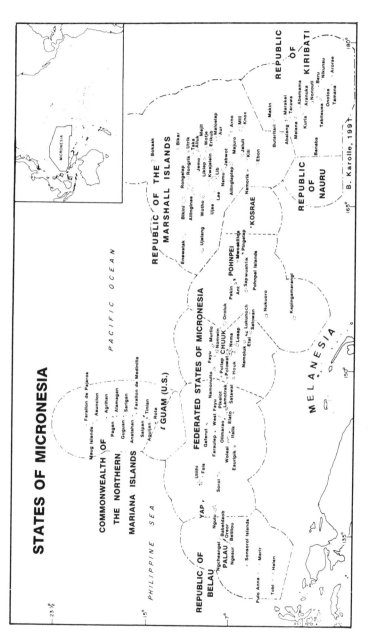

States of Micronesia (copyright B. Karolle)

ISLAND NAMES

Caroline Islands

Federated States of Micronesia
1. State of Kosrae
   Kosrae (Kusaie)

2. State of Pohnpei
   Pingelap
   Mwokil (Mokil)
   Pohnpei Islands (Ponape Islands)
      Pohnpei
      Ant
      Pakin
   Ngetick (Ngatik)
   Oroluk
   Minto Reef
   Nukuoro
   Kapingamarangi

3. State of Truk (Chuuk)
   Mortlock Islands (Namoi)
      Satawan
      Lukunor
      Etal
   Namokuk
   Losap
   Nama
   Hall Islands
      Murilo
      Nomwin
      Fayu
   Truk Islands (Chuuk)
      Moen (Wono)
      Dublon (Tonowas)

Gagil Tamil (Gagil-Tomil)
Yap
Ngulu

Republic of Belau

Belau (Palau Islands)
  Ngeruangel (Ngaruangl Reef)
  Ngcheangel (Kayangel)
  Babeldaob (Babelthuap)
  Oreor (Koror)
  Ngerekebesang (Arakabesan)
  Ngerchaol (Ngargol)
  Ngemelachel (Malakal)
  Chelbacheb (Rock Islands)
    Ulebsechel (Auluptagel)
    Ngeteklou (Gologugeul)
    Bukrrairong (Kamori)
    Ngeruktabel (Urukthapel)
    Tlutkaraguis (Adorius)
    Butottoribo
    Ongael
    Ngebedangel (Ngobasangel)
    Ulong (Aulong)
    Mercherchar (Eil Malk)
    Bablomekang (Abappaomogan)
    Ngerukeuid (Orukuizu)
  Ngemlis (Ngemelis Islands)
  Ngercheu (Ngergoi)
  Ngedbus (Ngesebus)
  Ngerechong (Ngeregong)
  Ngebad (Ngabad)
  Beliliou (Peleliu)
  Ngeaur (Angaur)

Belau Outliers
  Sonsorol Islands
    Fana
    Sonsoral
  Pulo Anna

Merir
Tobi
Helen (Helen Reef)

Gilbert Islands

Part of the Republic of Kiribati

Arorae
Tamana
Onotoa
Nikunau
Beru
Tabiteuea
Nonouti
Aranuka
Kuria

Abemama
Maina
Tarawa
Abaiang
Marakei
Butaritari
Makin (Little Makin)
Banaba (Ocean Island)

Mariana Islands

Territory of Guam
Guam

Commonwealth of the Northern Marianas Islands
Rota (Luta)
Aguijan
Tinian
Saipan
Farallon de Medinilla
Anatahan
Sarigan
Guguan
Alamagan
Pagan
Agrihan
Asuncion Island
Maug Islands
Farallon de Pajaros (Uracas)

Marshall Islands

Republic of the Marshall Islands

Ratak Chain	Ralik Chain
Bokaak (Taongi)	Ebon
Bikar	Namorik
Utrik (Utirik)	Kili
Taka	Jaluit
Mejit	Ailinglaplap (Ailinglapalap)
Ailuk	Jabwot
Jemo	Namu
Likiep	Lib
Wotje	Kwajelein
Erikub (Erikup)	Lae
Maloelap	Ujae
Aur	Wotho
Majuro	Rongrik (Rongerik)
Arno	Rongelap
Mili	Ailinginae
Knox (Narik)	Bikini
	Enewetak (Eniwetok)
	Ujelang

THE DICTIONARY

A

ALCOHOL IN THE PACIFIC The people of Oceania did not
make or consume alcoholic beverages of any sort prior to
European contact. Despite this, foreigners who came among
them wasted little time in introducing the islanders to
"Demon Rum." Following an initial rejection of liquor,
many islanders heartily embraced this new substance, an
embrace that led to a host of new problems in social control.
While beachcombers (q.v.), whalers, and traders were teaching Pacific islanders how to manufacture homemade liquors
and were selling them cheap commercial whiskey, missionaries were working just as hard to wean their converts away
from the "sinful excesses" of drunkenness. In much of
Oceania, abstinence from alcoholic beverages became an
important badge of Christian identity.

As colonial empires expanded into the Pacific, new laws
were enacted to control alcohol manufacture and consumption. In a few places, such as Abemama in the Gilberts,
locally imposed prohibitions on alcohol use were enforced
by traditional chiefs, but attempts at prohibition from within
were a rarity. By and large, none of these efforts at prohibition, colonial or otherwise, proved successful for very
long. In this respect the experience of Pacific islanders
echoes that of persons elsewhere in the world where official
efforts to stamp out alcohol use have been made and failed.
Sporadic attempts at total prohibition continue to be made
in parts in Oceania, but their likelihood of success is
dim.

Scholarly research on alcohol use and abuse in Oceania
has been limited in spite of the fact that alcoholism and
drunkenness are widely remarked to be major problems.
Studies completed by 1973 have been summarized and

1

reviewed and two bibliographies of publications on alcohol and kava (q.v.) use in the islands also are available. Only one full-scale ethnography of drinking behavior and drunken comportment in a Pacific society exists.

During the century or two that most Pacific islanders have had access to commercially produced alcoholic beverages or the knowledge of how to make their own, most alcohol consumed has been produced abroad and imported to the islands. Increasingly, however, commercial alcoholic beverage manufacture has become a part of island life. For example, local beers are brewed in Fiji, Western Samoa, French Polynesia, and Papua New Guinea, and both sake and pineapple wine (Maui Blanc) are made in Hawaii. (See also Betal nut chewing; Sakau)

AMERICAN BOARD OF COMMISSIONERS FOR FOREIGN MISSIONS (ABCFM) Patterned after other missionary groups such as the London Missionary Society, the ABCFM was active in Oceania after 1820, sending Congregational ministers, doctors, teachers, and farmers to the Pacific. In Micronesia, the ABCFM established missions at Kosrae, Pohnpei, and Ebon during the 1850s and at Chuuk in the 1870s. By the 1880s more than fifty ABCFM churches were in the Carolines and Marshalls. (See also Boston Mission Schools; Doane, Edward T.; Logan, Robert W.; *Morning Star* [ship]; Sturges, Albert)

ANSON, GEORGE (1697–1762) In 1740 Commodore George Anson received orders to lead a Royal Navy squadron, consisting of the *Centurion* and seven other vessels, to the Pacific to raid Spanish shipping. Off Cape Espiritu Santo in the Philippines he seized the richly laden galleon *Nuestra Senora de Cobagonda*. He returned to London in 1744.

In the course of his voyage he landed on Tinian in 1742 with a starving, thirsty crew. The water, fruit, and cattle on the island saved the Englishmen from death. Several of his crew members later wrote long, glowing accounts of their stay on Tinian. These were the first accounts of the Marianas published in English. Tinian and Saipan continued to be used as provisioning stops by ships passing through the Marianas because of these favorable reports. (See also: War of Jenkin's Ear)

ATKINS-KROLL COMPANY Established in Guam in 1914 as a branch of its main office in San Francisco by David Atkins and Clifton Kroll. Their main business was copra (q.v.) trading throughout Micronesia and the Philippines, and they operated several schooners and other sailing craft. The *Avarua* was the most famous of the AK ships that plied Micronesian waters. Atkins-Kroll had Guam's first commercial license in the American naval administration period. They also traded in dried goods and stocks from the mainland and brought to Guam the first radios, record players, and automobiles. In the 1970s Atkins-Kroll was taken over by the Inchcape Group, a British conglomerate, but it still operates on Guam as an automotive dealer.

ATOMIC TESTING See Nuclear Tests

B

BEACHCOMBERS The name collectively given to visitors, maroons, adventurers, and castaways who came to Micronesia during the eighteenth and nineteenth centuries, usually not of their choice. Charles Washington, an Englishman who jumped ship, was a beachcomber on Palau in the early nineteenth century and stayed for thirty years and claimed to be the sixth chief of Ngecherelong, Palau.

These beachcombers often were the only connection the islanders had to the outside world, and they frequently assisted traders and colonials in getting established in the islands due to the knowledge they had acquired of the local cultures. (See also O'Connell, James F.)

BECHE-DE-MER *Bêche-de-mer,* or trepang, as the seaslug is called, is found in the warm waters off many Micronesian islands. It was collected, then cleaned, boiled, and smoked in drying sheds. It was then shipped to the China markets where it could fetch between $500 and $1,000 per ton. Wealthy

Chinese paid well for this delicacy, which they used in soup. *Bêche-de-mer* was thought to be an aphrodisiac.

BERNART, LUELEN (1866–1946) The first Micronesian to write a history of a Micronesian island, Luelen Bernart was born of noble blood in the Kitti kingdom of Pohnpei Island. He attended the American Protestant mission school at Oa in Madolenihmw where he studied English, mathematics, geography, the Bible, and world history. Bernart's ability to read and write distinguished him from most Pohnpeians of his day. Plans to attend a religious seminary in Hawaii were dropped at the insistence of his parents. He then spent a good part of his life as a teacher in the mission schools and as an adviser and confidante to Henry Nanpei (q.v.), the most prosperous Micronesian businessman of the late nineteenth and early twentieth centuries. Bernart journeyed with Nanpei to Hong Kong and other Asian ports in 1896, a singular feat for Pohnpeians in those days. During the Japanese administration of the island, Bernart served with distinction as a village chief. At the time of his death, he held the title of Nansaurirrin, the third highest in the Naniken's or prime minister's line. The *Book of Luelen* was written over a twelve-year period from 1934 to 1946 in several school notebooks. The last nineteen chapters of the manuscript were dictated by a weakened Bernart to his daughter Sarihna. The book contains many of the legends, myths, chants, and magical spells that form the basis of Pohnpeian culture and tradition. Reflecting Bernart's early religious training, the book follows an orderly sequence of events, which, like the Bible, are divided into chapters and verses. The book offers a rough chronology of Pohnpeian times from the prehistoric migration of Pacific peoples to the German period (1900–1914). The *Book of Luelen* was discovered in 1947 by Saul Riesenberg, a former trust territory anthropologist and later senior ethnographer of the Smithsonian Institution. It was not until 1963, however, that Riesenberg was able to secure a copy. Fellow anthroplogists John L. Fischer and Marjorie G. Whiting assisted in the translation and editing of the manuscript.

BETEL NUT CHEWING The practice of chewing betel nut is characteristic of the Micronesian area but is most widely observed in Yap and Palau. The betel nut is picked rather green throughout the year. Small nuts are split open, some of the juicy center pulp removed with a knife or fingernail, and a pinch of lime (the caustic chemical) is added to the middle, after which the nut is wrapped in a piece of kebui leaf. Only one-half or one-third of the larger nuts are used at a time. Due to the scarcity of kebui, only a small portion is placed atop the lime part of the nut. Sometimes a piece of twist tobacco or cigarette is added. The combination is placed between the back molars and chewed.

The lime is white, the kebui green, and the betel nut is green-husked with a yellow or pinkish-yellow inside, but the juice one spits out when chewing the combination is a bright red. Evidently there is a factor in the betal nut-lime-kebui combination that acts as an indicator for alkali. The juice, when drooled on one's clothes, results in a stubborn stain that can be effaced by rubbing it immediately with lime (the fruit) juice, vinegar, or bleach.

Micronesians obtain lime by burning staghorn coral with hardwood. The calcium carbonate of the coral is converted to calcium hydroxide or quicklime. Too much lime in a chew can burn the mouth. Kebui, related to the pepper plant, is a creeping vine that grows around the trunks of tall, straight trees. When kebui is scarce, some villages require all persons who go about at night to identify themselves to a patrol whose members know where all kebui vines grow in the village and inspect them periodically. Rules apply to all persons within the village, and fines and punishments are levied on violators.

Claims that betel nut has narcotic properties are groundless. Frequent chewing of betel nuts causes the teeth to become red. After many years of chewing, if a person has been negligent in cleaning his teeth, they will become quite black. There is no evidence that betel nut chewing causes or enhances tooth decay. It may even be beneficial in that the frequent presence of alkali in the mouth may neutralize the acids produced by oral bacteria, which are responsible for tooth decay. Very old people who have lost most of their teeth carry a mortar and pestle with which they pulverize the ingredients of a chew before putting it in their mouth.

Some college parasitology texts state that the incidence of certain intestinal parasites among betel nut chewers is less than among nonchewers. This may be in part due to the possible effectiveness of the swallowed juice as a vermifuge and also to the fact that the constant spitting of chewers helps rid their throats of larval worms that otherwise would be swallowed.

Altogether, betel nut chewing in Micronesia is considered to be a healthful and pleasurable activity. (See also Alcohol in the Pacific; Sakau)

BLACKBIRDING The lowest point in the relations between Micronesians and foreigners during the nineteenth century was heralded by an ominous notice that appeared in the *Whaleman's Shipping List* in February 1869. It said that the "numerous groups of Micronesia are infested with a set of lawless men who are engaged in nothing more or less than the slave trade."

The statement pertained to "blackbirders," and just three years later the brig *Carl,* one of the most infamous black-birding ships in the Pacific, appeared in the Mortlocks and took eighty men off these islands to work in the plantations of Fiji. Another unidentified slave ship stopped there within two years of the *Carl* and carried away still more Mortlock-ese, this time to Samoa. It was not until 1881 that many of these laborers were returned home.

A foreign trader who resided at Lukunor Island at the time reports that eight men were brought back to that island aboard the schooner *Shanghai,* all decked out in European clothing and eager to tell of their adventures. Unfortunately, they had little opportunity to enjoy their release, he relates, for within four months all of them had died.

When the *HMS Blanch* sailed into Truk (Chuuk) lagoon in 1872 to investigate charges of murder and kidnapping against the *Carl,* its landing party found nothing but deserted houses and cooked breadfruit that the people of Tsis Island had left behind in their haste to escape and hide.

Whether or not this unwanted timidity on the part of the Trukese was due to a recent encounter with blackbirders, or simply to an instinctive fear of reprisals that they had developed, is not possible to discern. In any event, blackbirders were a scourge and a black mark on islander-foreigner visits of their time. (See Hayes, William Henry; Pease, Benjamin)

BLANCHARD, MADAN (1761–?) Blanchard was a member of British Captain Henry Wilson's *Antelope* crew, which was stranded on Palau in August 1783. The Palauans and Englishmen cooperated, built a new ship of mixed design, sailed off to Macao, and took with them the young Palauan prince Lee Boo (q.v.), who later died in England of smallpox.

In exchange, however, Captain Wilson left Madan Blanchard in Palau. Blanchard, in fact, volunteered to stay after high chief Ibedul promised him titled status, two wives, a house, and a plantation. He was about twenty, uneducated, and without trade skills, but nevertheless appeared "good tempered" and "inoffensive." Captain Wilson, before agreeing to leave Blanchard on Palau, tried to dissuade him, and after Blanchard passed this test, the Captain gave in and said that he "possessed courage in an eminent degree, a virtue held in high esteem by the natives of Palau."

Madan Blanchard had demonstrated his bravery a number of times during some expeditions against Koror's rivals. This may have brought him unexpected prestige. Perhaps he fancied himself as soon to be in the role of chief military adviser to the Ibedul.

Before Wilson left he reminded Blanchard of some essentials of English deportment: "Never go naked . . . support a superior character . . . keep the Sabbath . . . and perhaps most important, take care of the arms left with the *Ibedul*." But from that moment on, Blanchard went steadily downhill in Palau. He refused to work or fish, he took other people's food without permission, and even ran after other men's wives. This reportedly was tolerated for three years, and then one night, after some particularly demeaning outrage, several Palauan men ganged up on Blanchard and killed him. It was an unfortunate end to what might have been a rewarding exchange.

BORDALLO, BALTAZAR JEROME (1900–1984) Bordallo was a Guam businessman and politician. Born in Agat, he left Guam when he was fifteen to attend schools in the United States. He returned to the island in 1920 and established several small businesses. During the 1930s he served as chairman of the Guam Congress's (q.v.) House of Council. He is best remembered for his 1936 trip, with Francisco B. Leon Guerrero, to Washington, D.C., in an unsuccessful effort to have United States citizenship and civil rights extended to the people of Guam. He returned to the reactivated Guam Congress after World War II. He was elected to the first, second, and third Guam Legislatures (q.v.), and retired in 1956.

BORDALLO, RICARDO J. (1927–1990) Bordallo was a Guam businessman and politician, the son of Baltazar Jerome Bordallo (q.v.). Educated in Guam schools and the University of San Francisco, Bordallo was elected to the fourth, fifth, sixth, seventh, eighth, ninth, and tenth Guam Legislatures (q.v.). He also served as Chairman of Guam's Popular (now Democratic) Party from 1960 to 1963. Bordallo was elected governor of the territory in 1974 and again in 1982, the first governor of Guam to serve two terms in office. Charges of corruption tainted his second term. Facing a four-year prison term for witness tampering and conspiracy to obstruct justice, Bordallo committed suicide on 31 January 1990. He maintained that he was a victim of a politically motivated prosecution. Throughout his career Bordallo advocated broader home rule for Guam.

BOSTON MISSION SCHOOLS The Protestant missionaries from Boston, the American Board of Commissioners for Foreign Missions (ABCFM) (q.v.), first reached Micronesia in 1852. Hawaii had already been established with missions, and some native Hawaiians came to Micronesia to help establish the missions there. Schools were established at Kosrae, Pohnpei, and at many sites in the Marshalls.

In 1884 Reverend Robert W. Logan (q.v.) and his wife established the first mission schools at Truk (Chuuk). (See Doane, Edward T.; Sturges, Albert)

BRADLEY, WILLIS W., JR. (1884–1954) Bradley was governor of Guam from 1929–1931. Born in New York, Bradley was educated at the U.S. Naval Academy, receiving his commission in 1908. During World War I he was awarded the Congressional Medal of Honor for heroism aboard the *USS Pittsburg*. While governor, Bradley started the Guam postal system, gave the island residents a bill of rights, and pushed for U.S. citizenship for Guamanians. During his administration the writ of habeas corpus was applicable on Guam for the first time, women were enfranchised, the right of citizens to vote in general elections was established, and the Guam Congress (q.v.) was reorganized. He is remembered as the naval governor who did more for the civil rights and self-government of the people than any other. Bradley retired from the Navy in 1946, represented California's 18th district in Congress from 1947 to 1949, and was elected to the California State Assembly in 1952. He died while attending a legislative hearing.

C

CALVO, EDUARDO TORRES (1909–1963) Born in Agana, Calvo attended school on Guam before going to work for the Bank of Guam (q.v.) in 1926. In 1938 he began selling insurance; from this small start he built what is now Calvo Enterprises, which includes insurance, distribution, wholesale, real estate, and other concerns. He was elected to the Guam Congress (q.v.) in 1934. During the 1950s he was also elected to the first, second, and third Guam Legislatures (q.v.). Calvo founded the Territorial Party of Guam.

CAMACHO, CARLOS (1928–) First elected native Chamorro governor of the Commonwealth of the Northern Mariana Islands (CNMI) (q.v.) in 1977. Carlos Camacho was a medical officer and served for many years as a practicing physician in Saipan prior to his political career.

CAMACHO, CARLOS G. (1924–1979) Camacho was governor of Guam from 1969–1974. Born in Agana he attended Guam schools before studying at Aquinas College and Marquette University in the United States. After receiving his Doctor of Dental Surgery degree in 1952, Camacho joined the staff of Guam Memorial Hospital. He also served as a captain in the Dental Corps of the U.S. Army Reserve. He was elected to the eighth Guam Legislature (q.v.), and in 1969 was appointed governor of Guam by President Richard Nixon. He was the last appointed and first elected governor. In 1970 he successfully ran for the governorship with Kurt Moylan as his running mate. His administration was noted for public works projects, especially roads, bridges, and sewers, the expansion of Guam's international airport, and for an increase in tourism.

CANNIBALISM Traditionally, cannibalism was not practiced by the native peoples of Micronesia as far as is known, although it was practiced in the South Pacific in Fiji and elsewhere. During World War II, some Japanese military personnel were documented as practicing cannibalism on American and Australian prisoners. During the War Crimes Trials (q.v.) after World War II, some Japanese officers were accused of cannibalism, but the Allied Tribunal chose not to hear cases of cannibalism, but rather of the charge of murder, for which several Japanese were convicted and executed.

CANOES Traditional sailing craft—outrigger canoes—in Micronesia were some of the finest of their type ever known. In 1686 the Britisher William Dampier (q.v.) visited Guam and described Micronesian sailing canoes capable of navigating the 1,500 miles from Guam to Manila in just four days. He described their speeds as being in excess of twelve knots, which would place them among the most efficient sailing crafts in history.

All Micronesian canoes are of the outrigger type. Some are as long as fifty feet. Navigational methods and skills enable some to sail over great distances of open ocean; others, such as those from Palau, are adept at close-in maneuvering inside reefs.

Generally, the Micronesian canoes are double-ended dugouts with planked sides and a small deck. Sides are shaped with an adz and tied in place with sennit twine. The outrigger is lashed in place; no nails or metal fastenings of any kind are used, as this would destroy the canoe's flexibility, which allows it to withstand shocks of wave and current and reef action without breaking up.

The outrigger platform is designed to allow for lateral movement of the outrigger independent of the hull, much as in the independent suspension of a modern automobile.

Micronesian canoes lack the elaborate decoration of Polynesian and Melanesian canoes, all efforts being subordinated to the primary requirements of speed and performance in any sea conditions.

Normally the canoe hull is made of breadfruit or *mammea* logs, with mangrove and bamboo used for parts of the deck and outrigger assembly. Originally the sails were woven of pandanus fiber, though now canvas is most common. They are lateen sails suspended from a hinged mast, allowing the entire sail to be turned around to change the direction of the boat. The outrigger must remain on the windward side in order to prevent the sail from collapsing.

The prow is usually carved separately and lashed into place. Various prow types within each area or island group denote the canoes' use and status, although even here local variations can be noted. (See Stick Charts)

CAROLINE ISLANDS The largest archipelago in Micronesia, it stretches over 3,000 miles from Tobi Island at 131 degrees east longitude and four degrees north latitude and runs eastward to Kosrae Island at 162 degrees east longitude and five degrees north latitude. There are some 952 islands containing 452 square miles of land area. The 1990 estimated population was 200,000.

The Carolines are high and low volcanic and coral islands and atolls. Within the Carolines is the political entity of the Federated States of Micronesia (FSM) (q.v.), which is comprised of Truk (Chuuk), Yap, Pohnpei, and Kosrae. The Republic of Palau is a separate political entity, but it is also a part of the Carolines and is known as the western Carolines.

Carolingean people are brown, of medium stature, have straight to wavy black hair, high cheekbones, and little facial and body hair.

Vegetation varies from high islands to low atolls with coconut and breadfruit being common to both. Coral atolls abound in shore plants and pandanus. There are mangrove swamps on the high islands in the tidal flats, coconut palms on the slopes, and mixed forest growth on the uplands. Dogs, pigs, and rats were introduced by migrations prior to Western and Oriental contact. Domestic farm animals are present. There are many marine and shorebirds. Two species of saltwater crocodiles are found in Palau, as well as monkeys introduced by the Japanese.

Carolinians are Micronesians with the exception of some Polynesian strains at Kapingamarangi and Nukuoro Atolls in the eastern Carolines. Anthropological evidence indicates that Carolinians probably originated in Southeast Asia and Malaysia. Carolinian societies are similar in cultural characteristics and adjustment to small island living. (See Canoes; Coordinated Investigation of Micronesian Anthropology)

CHAMORRO AGRICULTURAL PRACTICES Chamorro farmers during Spanish times had some agricultural superstitions that have been demonstrated to have some basis in scientific fact. They held that the growing of seeds and flowering plants was helped by the moonlight and so they often planted by the phases of the moon.

Then, about fifty years ago some experiments were done by botanists in England that suggested that the Chamorros and other island peoples of the Pacific certainly had something good with regard to planting by the moonlight. These British experiments showed that the germination of seeds is indeed hastened by the action of polarized light and that the moonlight is partly this type of light.

Guam farmers hold that if sweet potatoes, yams, and other tuber crops are planted at low tide, and full moon, they will bear greater returns in number, but small in size. If you plant when the tide is high and the moon is full, however, the fields will probably not produce so many, but the crop will be larger in size and better in quality.

A traditional explanation for growing ground crops is that when the tide is low there are many rocks and stones in view on the reef. Ground plants, such as those just mentioned, set out at this time will produce a crop that will cause the fields to be covered with potatoes and other products that grow on the ground. Such planting is very often traditionally done at night when the tide and moon are favorable.

Sometimes the Chamorro farmers could not actually explain why they planted in the manner they did, but still they got results, results that are time-honored and now demonstrated to have some scientific basis.

CHAMORRO EDUCATION (JESUIT) The early education of the Chamorros by the Jesuits was not based on cultural understanding, tactfulness, and love. With little understanding and appreciation of the native culture, the Jesuits thrust Christian concepts of religious, moral, and social values upon the Chamorros. Confined and herded together like animals on Guam, the old ways were increasingly condemned. The Chamorros were forced to give up their ancestor worship, warfare, bachelor houses, and most of the indigenous ceremonies, including chanting and dancing, and were compelled to replace them with Spanish Catholic rituals. (See San Juan de Letran; Spanish Mission Schools)

CHAMORRO WARS Also referred to as Spanish-Chamorro Wars, they were a series of violent conflicts between the Chamorros of the Marianas and the Spanish missionary colonials, which are generally taken to have started with the martyring of Father Diego Luis de Sanvitores (q.v.) in 1668 and ended with the final subjugation of the Chamorros under the authority of the Spanish Crown by Don Jose de Quiroga (q.v.) in 1695.

CHAMORROS The precontact inhabitants of the Mariana Islands (q.v.) were the ancient Chamorros. These pre-Spanish, proto-Malayan people had settled the islands probably as long as 3,000 to 5,000 years ago. Their point of origin is obscure; probably from the Philippines and Southeast Asia. There is some evidence that a people with a rice culture invaded the Marianas around A.D. 800 and brought also the *latte* stone (q.v.) technology. *Latte* stones were huge pillars and capstones used as supports for houses.

The Chamorros were organized into matrilineal clans. Marriage was monogamous with divorced permitted. Children became members of the mother's clan and had little contact with the paternal side of the family.

In addition the society was organized into a two-tiered caste system. The upper castes consisted of two groups, the *matua* and the *atchoat*. The *matua* possessed most of the privileges and wealth within the society. *Matua* who broke society's rules became *atchoat*. Members of the lower caste were known as the *manachang*. According to Spanish accounts, they lived like slaves and were set apart from the rest of the society.

The economic system consisted of gardening, gathering, and fishing. Rice was cultivated as a ceremonial food. The Chamorros were skilled craftsmen and produced a variety of articles in stone, shell, bone, wood, clay, and other raw materials available. Trade was carried out throughout the island chain using shell money as a medium of exchange. Within the society, economic relations were characterized by reciprocity and conspicuous display.

Religious beliefs are obscure; they apparently venerated the spirits of the dead called *aniti*. There were shamans and sorcerers. There was a group of herb doctors known by the Spanish terms *suruhano* and *suruhana*. (See Chamorro Agricultural Practices)

CHEYNE, ANDREW (1817–1866) Cheyne was a Scottish trader. Born in the Shetland Islands, Cheyne was trading in the Pacific by 1840. He first entered Micronesia in 1841 as supercargo of the *Diana*. Over the next six years he made several trips from Sydney through Melanesia to Pohnpei, Guam, and Palau. Cheyne returned to Scotland in 1848. Between 1852 and 1854, he circumnavigated the globe. He later returned to the Pacific engaging in various trading enterprises in New Guinea and Palau. He was killed at Koror in Palau in February 1866. The journals of his 1841–1844 voyages are full of valuable ethnographic and historical information.

CHINA CLIPPER China Clipper was the name given to the Martin 130 seaplanes that were flown by Pan American

Airways in the late 1930s between San Francisco and Manila. They carried passengers and mail. The first flight took place in November 1935. Guam was a regular stop for the *China Clippers,* the planes landing in Apra Harbor on the west coast of the island.

CLIMATE Temperatures are uniformly high year-round and rainfall is well distributed. The Marshalls, Carolines, and Marianas are drier from December to April, while the Gilberts get less rainfall from July to November. Kosrae and Pohnpei are among the rainiest placest on Earth. The Gilberts are much drier and have been known to experience drought. The main typhoon season in Micronesia is in the rainy season from July to December, although typhoons can occur at any time of year.

COMMANDER, NAVAL FORCES, MARIANAS (COM-NAVMAR) The overall U.S. naval authority in the western Pacific. A flag rank officer is designated commander and is directly responsible to the Commander-in-Chief, Pacific Area Command (CinCPAC), another flag officer, in Pearl Harbor, Hawaii. COMNAVMAR is a coordinated command. The commanding officer is also a representative to the autonomous governments in the region, including the Republic of Palau (q.v.), the Commonwealth of the Northern Mariana Islands, (q.v.) the Federated States of Micronesia (q.v.), and the Republic of the Marshall Islands (q.v.).

COMMONWEALTH OF THE NORTHERN MARIANA IS-LANDS (CNMI) Comprised of all the Mariana Islands (q.v.) except Guam, which is an unincorporated territory of the United States. The main islands are Saipan, Tinian, Rota, and Pagan; the population was about 23,000 in 1990. From 1922–1944 the CNMI was a part of the Japanese mandated islands from the League of Nations and was heavily populated by Japanese nationals. The Japanese developed the islands economically with agriculture, fisheries, and phosphate mining (q.v.). Native Chamorros were seen as ''last class'' citizens.

The United States wrested the islands from the Japanese in a series of bloody battles in World War II. After the war the Marianas became part of the Trust Territory of the Pacific

Islands (q.v.), a United Nations trusteeship administered by the United States. In 1955 the Central Intelligence Agency (CIA) established a training facility at Saipan, which was closed in 1962. The headquarters of the Trust Territory government moved to Saipan and occupied the former CIA facility as a headquarters where they remained until 1991.

Negotiations toward a future political status for the Northern Marianas (excluding Guam) started with the United States in 1969. In 1973 the Northern Marianas began separate negotiations with the United States toward a status of commonwealth. In 1975 the people of the Northern Marianas held a plebiscite and voted for a covenant for a commonwealth. In 1977 the constitution was approved and ratified and the first elected governor, Carlos Camacho (q.v.), took office on 9 January 1978.

COMMUNITY COLLEGE OF MICRONESIA The Community College of Micronesia (CCM) was formally established as a college in 1970 by an executive order from the High Commissioner of the Trust Territory of the Pacific Islands. The college grew out of a teacher-training program that had been called the Micronesian Teacher Education Center (MTEC). In 1977 the CCM became accredited by the Western States Commission on Junior and Community Colleges, and also became part of the College of Micronesia system, which was comprised of the CCM Nursing School (q.v.), located at Saipan, and the Micronesian Occupational College (q.v.), a vocational facility in Palau. The college system is governed by an eleven-member board of regents and is presided over by a chancellor. Enrollment, including extension programs throughout Micronesia, is over 1,300.

COMMUNITY COLLEGE OF MICRONESIA NURSING SCHOOL Part of the Community College of Micronesia (q.v.), the CCM Nursing School began at Saipan in 1969. It became part of the College of Micronesia system in 1977, and in 1990 it was moved to Majuro, Marshall Island Republic. The school trains nurses for all of Micronesia and enrolled over 200 students in 1992. (See Micronesian Occupational College)

COMPACTS OF FREE ASSOCIATION The Compacts of Free Association are negotiated documents—treaties, in effect, that govern the relationship between the new states of Micronesia and the United States. There are three separate Compacts; one each for (1) the Federated States of Micronesia (FSM) (q.v.); (2) the Republic of the Marshall Islands (RMI) (q.v.); and (3) the Republic of Palau (ROP) (q.v.). Each has to be approved in plebiscite by the electorate of each political entity. The Compacts for FSM and the RMI were approved and went into force in 1986. The Palau Compact is scheduled for implementation in late 1994.

CONGRESS OF MICRONESIA Established in 1965 by an executive order from the U.S. Secretary of the Interior, the Congress of Micronesia was seen largely as an educational program. The Congress was patterned after that of the United States with a Senate and House of Representatives. There were two senators elected from each Trust Territory district for four-year terms. There were six districts from 1965 to 1975 and then seven districts from 1975 until the end of the trusteeship in 1986. Representatives were elected for two-year terms and their numbers were based on population in similar fashion to the U.S. Congress. The Congress of Micronesia was able to pass revenue bills to raise taxes and then could allocate the funds from the collected taxes. The Congress, however, could not override the veto of the American High Commissioner and therefore could not allocate funds appropriated by the U.S. government without full concurrence of the High Commissioner. The Congress of Micronesia was a very successful educative body and many members of the autonomous legislatures subsequent to the Trust Territory government had previously served in the Congress of Micronesia.

COORDINATED INVESTIGATION OF MICRONESIAN ANTHROPOLOGY (CIMA) In 1942, shortly after World War II started in the Pacific, the Americans on the home front began to prepare for their eventual victory over Imperial Japan and their postwar responsibilities.

In the case of Micronesia, which prior to the Pacific war was a League of Nations mandate administered by Japan, a large research project was gotten under way to find out as much as possible about the islands and their people, which was available in library and archival sources.

As soon as the war ended, the United States began the Coordinated Investigation of Micronesian Anthropology known as CIMA—to undertake practical fieldwork in the islands with which to complement the library research that started during the war. In effect, CIMA was a large-scale social science research project that was coordinated by the Pacific Science Board of the National Academy of Sciences and funded by the U.S. Navy. Forty-two investigators were sent to study various aspects of traditional and contemporary Micronesian cultures. The project was for the purpose of helping the Navy provide effective and humane administration in the islands. The completed reports of the scientists covered such diverse topics as material culture, language, geography, traditional politics, and rehabilitation problems.

CIMA provided a great deal of information that has since proved to be very helpful in increasing the understanding between the cultures of the islands and the Americans.

COPRA No other western economic activity has touched the lives of so many Pacific islanders as has the copra trade. Coconut palms grow on all but the most forbidding atolls. Copra is made by opening the nuts and spreading out the white meat in large chunks to dry in the sun for several days. Sometimes it is dried in ovens. Then it is bagged in 100-pound burlap sacks. This process is simple enough for even the most technologically unsophisticated and remote islanders. Production requires hardly any investment capital. Moreover, copra has drawn outsiders—traders, planters, and their governments to places where few would have otherwise gone. From its rise to importance in the late nineteenth century, copra has provided the main export for most of the Pacific world. The Philippines, Indonesia, Sri Lanka, and Malaysia have been the largest producers, but in Oceania copra's impact has been greater and more rapidly apparent. Life in many areas of the island world of the Pacific has been, and continues to be, dominated by copra.

European demand created the trade. By the 1860s supplies of animal fats were insufficient to meet rising needs. Lacking America's ready source of cottonseed oil, Europeans turned to tropical vegetable oils. Many proved to be cheaper than animal fats even with the added cost of transportation. Of them, coconut oil was easily the most important. It went into soaps, margarine, explosives, and other products. By 1910 coconut oil, although still largely unknown in the United States, was widely used in Europe despite the opposition of the dairy and cattle industries.

On Guam, copra production was a big industry during the early period of the American administration. There were many growers. Mr. J. K. Shimizu operated a large tract of 18,000 trees. The Atkins-Kroll Company (q.v.) had the largest plantation at Tarague Beach with some 30,000 trees.

CORMORAN, SMS From 1899 to 1914 all of the islands of Micronesia except the Gilberts and Guam were colonized by Germany. The Germans had six field trip patrol ships that serviced the region. One of these was the cruiser *SMS Cormoran.* During World War I, before the United States became involved, the *Cormoran* sought refuge in Apra Harbor from the pursuing Japanese cruiser *Iwate.* The time was December 1914, and Japan had already entered the war against Germany.

The *Cormoran*'s thirty-three officers and 340 enlisted men outnumberd the U.S. Marines ashore, but there were no hostilities, and the *Cormoran,* running dangerously low on coal and food, was grateful for the safe harbor. Immediately she was interned and the Germans became semipermanent "guests." They were shortly granted post-exchange privileges and all other perks afforded officers and men of the U.S. Navy. The band gave concerts ashore; the German and American naval officers invited each other to various social affairs. All bills for the German's food and essentials were forwarded to the U.S. State Department in Washington, which was then reimbursed by the German Embassy.

On 6 April 1917, the United States declared war on Germany. Guam Governor Captain Roy C. Smith was informed of the action by cable and immediately demanded the surrender of the *Cormoran*. But instead of surrendering their ship, the Germans exploded charges in her coal bunkers to scuttle the warship with the loss of nine crewmen. One U.S. Marine fired his rifle in the encounter, and this became the first American-German hostile action of World I. The *Cormoran* sank in 120 feet of water in Apra Harbor where she rests today as a continuing attraction for scuba divers. Resting also on Guam are six of the *Cormoran*'s crew who are buried in the naval cemetery in Agana.

CORTE, FELIPE MARIA DE LA Corte was Governor of Guam from 1855–1866. Corte was an educated and intelligent man who worked to improve Guam's economic conditions. He wrote an interesting memoir of the island, which was published in Spain in 1875. His first year in office witnessed the last of Spain's annual subsidies to the government of Guam and a devastating smallpox epidemic. He recommended importing Chinese and Caroline islanders to replace those who had perished in the epidemic. A dispute he had with the United States consul led to a port call by the *USS Vandalia*. Corte was relived at his own request in 1866. (See Masters, Samuel J.)

D

DAMPIER, WILLIAM (1652–1715) William Dampier was a swashbuckling type of explorer, and he visited the Marianas in 1686, not twenty years after the Spanish had founded their first permanent colony at Agana, Guam. Dampier also visited Guam again in 1686 and 1710 with Woodes Rogers (q.v.). He was born in England and orphaned as a young boy. He followed various pursuits as a young man, including fighting in the Dutch War of 1673, cutting logs in Honduras, and later becoming a plantation manager in Jamaica. But soon he became a committed bucaneer and went on several expeditions against the Spanish in the New World.

He came to the Marianas with Captain Swan as part of a buccaneering voyage. They rounded Cape Horn and entered the Pacific with the idea of attacking Spanish towns on the west coast of South America. It was after these forays that they headed across the Pacific toward the Philippines and came to the Marianas. They pushed on to Mindanao where Dampier and Swan parted company.

Finally, following a series of curious adventures and unexpected misfortunes, including being marooned in the Nicobar Islands, William Dampier returned to England in 1691. Several years later he published an important book, *A New Voyage Round the World,* together with a supplemental volume, *Voyages and Descriptions.* These works were a significant contribution to exploration because of their sea lore and explanations of various places.

Eventually Dampier became a British naval officer and went on several other voyages for his country and became a fairly rich man before he died in March 1715 at St. Stephen Parish, London. (See Canoes)

DOANE, EDWARD T. Edward T. Doane was one of the early Protestant missionaries who arrived at Pohnpei in 1855, only three years after the mission was established. In 1857 he and his wife were posted at Ebon in the Marshall Islands where they remained for the next thirty years with only two home leaves for medical reasons. As a widower, Reverend Doane returned to the Pohnpei station in 1885 and became the senior member.

In 1887 Doane became a cause célèbre in some American newspapers because of a diplomatic dispute involving Catholic and Protestant missionary rivalries and the mission's land rights on Pohnpei. Pope Leo XIII intervened and arbitrated the dispute between Germany and Spain over rights to the Caroline Islands by giving Spain sovereignty and Germany freedom to trade. Spain had also been assured that the Protestant mission efforts would be allowed to continued.

In 1887 Don Posadillo, the newly appointed Spanish governor, arrived to establish a station on land at Kolonia. This area had been deeded to the mission by Pohnpeian chiefs, but Reverend Doane had agreed to make a portion of it available to the Spanish. Shortly thereafter, Doane formally protested Spanish encroachment on other parts of the mission land and was arrested on 13 April 1887 for disrespectful behavior.

Reverend Doane was deported to Manila but there gained a pardon from the governor-general and soon returned to Pohnpei where he found that governor Posadillo had been killed in a rebellion along with a number of Spanish soldiers. The difficulties continued and Reverend Doane finally left Pohnpei in 1889 without their complete resolution. The mission closed altogether in the following year and did not reopen for a whole decade. (See American Board of Commissioners for Foreign Missions; Boston Mission Schools; Logan, Robert W.; *Morning Star*; Sturges, Albert)

DUENAS, JESUS BAZA (1914–1944) Born on Guam, Duenas studied under Jesuit priests in Manila. He returned to Guam in 1938. During the Japanese occupation of the island (1941–1944) Duenas administered to the needs of the people who lived in the southern part of the island. He looked out for the welfare of the people, and this often brought him in conflict with the Japanese authorities. On 2 July 1944, just nineteen days before the start of the American recapture of Guam, he was arrested, tortured, and beheaded by the Japanese.

DUMONT D'URVILLE, JULES SEBASTIAN CESAR (1790–1842) Jules Sebastian Cesar Dumont D'Urville was a French explorer who visited Micronesia in 1828 and in 1837–1838. Born in 1790, Dumont D'Urville's first Pacific voyage was with his friend and colleague Louis Isidore Duperrey (q.v.) from 1822–1825. His next two voyages were entirely planned and executed by himself. The first was in 1826, and on it he continued explorations while at the same time searching for his lost countryman, Laperouse. He visited Australia, New Zealand, Fiji, and the Loyalty Islands, New Guinea, Guam, and the Carolines.

Everywhere he charted new coastlines and collected scientific data. Dumont D'Urville is quite famous and remembered for this scientific work. He found Laperouse's shipwreck site, a fact that was later confirmed by other explorers.

It was in 1834 that 24 volumes of his work appeared in print. Dumont D'Urville's second voyage is generally regarded as the last great French voyage of discovery. He set out to explore the southern polar regions and left France in 1837. He pushed far south but was stopped by polar ice caps in front of Antartica. Dumont D'Urville then zigzagged northward across the Pacific and stopped, going other places, at the Marianas and also the Carolines before going back to Antartica for one more try. Being unsuccessful, he then went home by way of New Zealand.

After returning home Dumont D'Urville edited his massive 24 volumes into a final publication of ten volumes, which became classics of Pacific exploration. Dumont D'Urville was promoted to rear admiral in the French navy in 1840 at the age of fifty. Two years later he died unexpectedly in a railroad accident.

DUPERREY, LOUIS-ISIDOR (1786–1865) Duperrey was a French explorer who took part in two scientific expeditions to the Pacific, both of which visited Micronesian islands. He served as Louis-Claude de Saulces de Freycinet's (q.v.) first lieutenant on that explorer's 1817–1820 voyage. Upon his return to France he was placed in charge of his own expedition sailing in the *Coquille* in 1822. He would be gone for almost three years. In May and June 1824 he was in the Gilberts and Carolines. His most valuable contribution was the description of Kosrae in his journal.

E

EARHART, AMELIA (1898–1937) Earhart was the first woman pilot to attempt to fly around the world, and she was lost over the South Pacific on her unsuccessful flight in July 1937. The testimony of various Micronesian islanders, responding to Western investigators' queries, have placed her disappearance in Micronesia.

Earhart announced plans to fly around the world in September 1936. She intended to use an equatorial route, and Howland Island in the south Pacific was the key to getting across the vast expanse of water. The government built the runways she would use on Howland, and with the help of the Army and the Works Progress Administration, these were finished in March 1937. Then, starting at Miami, Florida, in June, Earhart flew from west to east to avoid the Asian monsoons. She hopped through the Caribbean to Brazil, then across the Atlantic to Dakar, Senegal. Africa was crossed in easy stages followed by a long jump to Karachi, Pakistan. A series of short flights brought her down to Indonesia, where she stopped for a while due to mechanical trouble. Then she flew to Darwin, Australia, and on up to Lae, Papua New Guinea. There her plane, a Lockheed Electra—the fastest of her time—was overhauled for the 1,800-mile flight to Howland Island.

Earhart took off from Lae on 2 July and was tracked easily for about twelve hours. A long period of silence followed. Twenty hours into the flight she was heard from for the last time, but she never acknowledged receiving the countless radio messages sent.

Because of the assistance she received from the government, there has been speculation that she was a spy and deviated from her set course to overfly Japanese bases in the Caroline and Marshall Islands. Some say the Japanese caught her. In the late 1950s and early 1960s, Frederick A. Goerner, an investigative journalist, interviewed Micronesians at Saipan who contended that they saw her in a Saipan prison around the time of her disappearance. These allegations have never been proved, however.

ELLIS, EARL HANCOCK "PETE" Lt. Colonel Earl H. Ellis was the first American to penetrate Japanese-held Micronesia in 1923. A military tactician and planner, Ellis was stationed on Guam in 1914 and was head of the Guam Insular Patrol. In 1915 he and a small group of Marines took a three-inch gun across the reef off Orote Point and thus demonstrated for the first time that artillery could be landed from boats.

In 1920 Ellis went to Marine headquarters in Washington, D.C., to work on war plans and there completed his now famous 30,000 word report, "Advanced Base Operations in

Micronesia,'' a prophetic document that predicted WWII and outlined step-by-step the island bases that would have to be seized in order to take American seapower within striking distance of Japan. Ellis was able to see that Japanese control of Micronesia would make war with the U.S. inevitable, and twenty-three years later the Navy followed every essential of Ellis's plan.

In 1921 Ellis came to the Pacific under the guise of a commercial traveler and set out to spy and reconnoiter the best sites for American advanced bases. He visited Australia, Samoa, Fiji, the Philippines, and went on to Japan where he became ill from chronic alcoholism. He was then ordered home but instead pushed on through the Marshalls and Carolines, making detailed maps and charts. At Koror he became gravely ill from his continued drinking and died on 12 May 1923.

Colonel Ellis was one of the most brilliant Marine officers of his day, and his death was a great loss for the American military authorities at the time.

ENIWETOK, BATTLE OF, 1944 After the American capture of Kwajalein (q.v.) in early February 1944, Admiral Chester Nimitz (q.v.) ordered an immediate attack on Eniwetok in the western Marshalls. The landing took place on 17 February, and the island was secured within three days.

ENOLA GAY Enola Gay was the name of the American B-29 heavy bomber that dropped the first atomic bomb on Japan during World War II. The plane flew from North Field on Tinian in the Marianas on its mission to Hiroshima. The *Enola Gay* was named after the mother of the pilot, Paul Tibbets, Jr.

F

FEDERATED STATES OF MICRONESIA (FSM) A confederation of island groups in Micronesia, formerly a part of the Trust Territory of the Pacific Islands (TTPI) (q.v.). They are comprised of the following groups: Truk (Chuuk), Yap,

Kosrae, and Pohnpei. In 1978 they ratified a constitution and in 1986 became autonomous and freely associated with the United States through a Compact of Free Association (q.v.). (See Federated States of Micronesia, Constitution of)

FEDERATED STATES OF MICRONESIA, CONSTITUTION OF The Constitution was adopted in a United Nations-observed referendum on 12 July 1978, by the districts of Yap, Kosrae, Pohnpei, and Chuuk (Truk) of the Trust Territory of the Pacific Islands. The districts of Palau and the Marshalls rejected the Constitution and formed their own autonomous governments under their own constitutions.

The Constitution of the Federated States of Micronesia was written by a convention held between 12 July and 8 November 1975, on Saipan, Mariana Islands. It was made up of delegates from Yap, Pohnpei, Chuuk, the Marshalls, Palau, and the Northern Marianas. Sixty delegates were authorized, including twelve traditional leaders, six members of the Congress of Micronesia, and forty-two delegates elected from the districts by population. The Mariana and the Marshalls districts failed to send their full delegations. The convention was chaired by Tosiwo Nakayama (q.v.) of Chuuk, with University of Hawaii Professor of Political Science Norman Meller heading up the staff.

After the Constitution was written, the Northern Marianas separated from the rest of the Trust Territory through the adoption of their own covenant to establish a commonwealth with the United States and their own constitution in 1976. Kosrae became a separate district on 1 January 1977, thus replacing the Northern Marianas as the sixth district at the 12 July 1978 constitution referendum.

The Constitution established a presidential government with parliamentary overtones and a decentralized federal structure. The central government consists of a president and vice president, a congress of the Federated States, and a supreme court. The president and vice president are elected from the congressional membership elected at large, one from each of the four member states. The congress is composed of two types of senators: one from each state elected at large for a four-year term; and ten elected on the basis of population, one each from Kosrae and Yap, three from Pohnpei, and five from Chuuk, all for two-year terms. In order to balance the large and small districts, all legislation will be passed on second reading by each district delegation casting one vote.

The national government is restricted in its authority to international affairs, matters involving more than one state, and those "of a national character." Its taxing authority is restricted to import and income taxes. The district governments retain all other powers. A bill of rights is included in the Constitution guaranteeing the civil liberties of the citizens, protecting traditions and customs, and universal adult suffrage is provided. Each district or state is guaranteed its own constitution in conformity with provisions of the national constitution. In addition, states have exclusive rights over land matters in recognition of the importance of land in these small islands. The right of eminent domain is not mentioned at all in the national constitution.

The Constitution defines the boundaries of the Federated States to be twelve miles from an archipelagic baseline with an exclusive economic zone extending to 200 miles. An added provision, however, permits adjustments of this line to conform with international treaties of the Law of the Sea. In fact, instead of the archipelagic principle, each island now has a three-mile territorial water boundary, a twelve-mile exclusive fisheries zone, and an additional 188-mile fisheries jurisdiction.

States control resources within the twelve-mile zone, and the national government controls the 188 miles with a 50 percent revenue-sharing principle applying to the contiguous state and the national government for any returns on exploitation of the waters between twelve and 200 miles.

Political status is not dealt with directly in the national constitution, although independence is the basic theme. A status less than independence is provided for in Article IX, Section 4, which permits the delegation of major governmental authorities to another government with the consent of two-thirds of the state legislatures. This provision has been accepted as compatible with the principle of free association with the United States, which is the negotiated status; and it was in force when the trusteeship with the United Nations was terminated in 1986.

The Constitution became partially effective on 12 July 1979, one year following the referendum, in those states that ratified it. It became fully effective upon the termination of the Trusteeship Agreement.

The first Congress of the Federated States was elected on 27 March 1979, with the election of the executive branch in mid May following the organization of the congress beginning in 10 May at the new capital of the Federated States in Pohnpei.

FLORES, FELIXBERTO CAMACHO (1921–1985) Born in Agana, Flores attended the Guam Institute before entering Ateneo de Manila, a Jesuit-run institution in the Philippines, in 1939. He transferred to the San Jose Seminary, also in the Philippines, the following year. Flores completed his theological studies at St. John's Seminary in Massachusetts in 1949. He was ordained a priest that same year and was consecrated a bishop in 1970. In 1984 Flores was appointed the first archbishop of Agana.

FLORES, JOSE AGUON (1859–1940) Born in Agana, Flores joined the Congregational church established on Guam in 1901 by Dr. Francis M. Price, an American Board of Commissioners for Foreign Missions (q.v.) missionary. He was ordained a minister in 1906 by Price and Reverend E. B. Case. Flores was the first Chamorro Protestant minister.

FLORES, JOSEPH (1900–1981) Flores was a Guam businessman, publisher, and politician. He was the first Chamorro to serve as governor of Guam, serving from 1960–1961. Flores left Guam during World War I while he served in the U.S. Navy. He remained in California, where he became a successful businessman until 1947. In 1950 he became the owner, editor, and publisher of the *Guam Daily News*. In 1954 he founded the Guam Savings and Loan Association, the first privately owned financial institution chartered on Guam. During his brief administration he urged American leaders to provide for the election of Guam's governor and for a Guam delegate to the United States Congress.

FLORES, NIEVES M. (1890–1949) Flores was a Guam educator. Born in the Philippines, Flores was educated in private and public schools, graduating from Manila High School in 1920. Two years later he was loaned to the government of Guam as a surveyor. He remained on Guam, founding the Guam Institute, a private school, in 1923. Guam's central public library in Agana is named in his honor.

FOLK MEDICINES Native medicines in Micronesia continue to have great importance, especially to people living in remote areas. The earliest histories of the Marianas mention the use of medicinal herbs. Methods for the use and preparation of the medicines are handed down through generations. These people who inherit the special knowledge are selected by a long process of consensus, and in some cases they might be members of the immediate family or close relatives.

Because, traditionally, knowledge is private rather than public property in Micronesia, the act of passing along knowledge about traditional medicines is secret, and the ingredients, proportions, and special preparations are not disclosed to outsiders as a rule. The practitioners are often called witch doctors, although probably the term ''herb doctor'' is more appropriate. Throughout Micronesia there appear to be three classes of healers for three types of illnesses: those caused by sorcery, those caused by spirits and ghosts, and those of natural causes.

Plants are the origin of most ingredients for local medicines, and botanists describing the flora of the region may frequently refer to the medicinal properties of plants. Some ethnobotanists and anthropologists have reported specific illnesses, medicinal ingredients, and methods of preparation and application that are used in healing efforts in the islands.

Sometimes islanders regard members of the Western medicinal professions with suspicion, perhaps because herb doctors are not licensed and work outside of legally acceptable practice. The traditional island ways with home remedies may have even more significance for modern medicine in the future.

FOREIGN INVESTMENT Since 1945, when the United States first began administering the scattered islands in the 3 million square miles of western Pacific Ocean known as the Trust Territory of the Pacific Islands (q.v.) (Micronesia), foreign investment has been strongly regulated. From 1945 to 1974, foreign investment was allowed only by American citizens under the United States administration's interpretation of Article 8 of the United Nations Trusteeship Agreement, "the most favored nation" clause. In 1974 the Secretary of the Interior reversed this policy in an attempt to attract other members of the community of nations to invest. As of 1979 the bulk of foreign investment in Micronesia remained that owned by U.S. citizens.

Under the military naval administration of the territory (1945–1951), policy on foreign investment was promulgated by a directive with the aim of keeping the inhabitants of Micronesia from being exploited by any outside interests. Under the Department of the Interior administration, which began in 1951, a code of laws was promulgated that continued the Navy's regulations of business. In 1962 a major policy change allowed U.S. citizen investment, but limited other investment in Micronesia to less than ten businesses, most of which were owned by persons who had lived and done business in Micronesia under the Japanese administration.

In 1970 the Congress of Micronesia (q.v.) enacted the Foreign Investors Business Permit Act, which provided a general formula under which foreign investment applications can be screened and business permits issued. The act is regulatory in nature and does not provide development incentives.

Foreign investment in Micronesia had remained at about $17 to $18 million in its entities, excluding the Northern Marianas, since 1973. With the establishment of a separate government in the Northern Marianas in 1978, U.S. individuals or companies are no longer required to obtain foreign business permits. The area with the most significant growth, outside of the Marianas, had been Palau, which increased its investments by $5 million during the last half of the 1970s.

The Trusteeship Agreement under which Micronesia was administered until 1986 applies currently only to Palau, which is the last remaining United Nations trusteeship. The governments of the Commonwealth of the Northern Mariana Islands, the Marshalls, and the Federated States of Micronesia are now separate entities. The strict regulatory policies, laws, and regulations that have been in force for many years have been continued by these new governments, with the exception of the Northern Marianas. There, liberal investment policies for foreigners are encouraged to promote a lively tourism industry.

FREYCINET, LOUIS-CLAUDE DE SAULCES DE (1779–1842) Freycinet was a French explorer who commanded an expedition to the Pacific in 1817–1820. His first lieutenant was Louis-Isidor Duperrey (q.v.). In 1819 Freycinet, in the *Uranie,* visited the Carolines and Guam, spending eleven weeks at that Spanish colony. The *Uranie* was shipwrecked in the Falkland Islands on her return to France; the scientific data and specimens on board were saved, however. Both Freycinet and his wife, Rose, who had been smuggled aboard disguised as a sailor, published accounts of the voyage.

G

GERMAN SOUTH SEAS EXPEDITION A two-year-long survey of the cultures of the islanders in Micronesia from 1908–1910 when they were under the German administration. This expedition was funded by the *Hamburgische Wissenschaftliche Stiftung* (Hamburg Science Foundation). Approval for the expedition was given on 20 December 1907, and the party left as of 15 May 1908. Dr. Georg Thilenius of the *Hamburgische Museum fuer Voelkerkunde* (Hamburg Museum of Ethnology) directed the expedition and the publication of its results. Rabaul, New Guinea, was chosen for the base of the operations.

Five trips were made from August 1908 until June 1909 to the Admiralty and Hermit Islands, New Britain, along the northeastern coast of New Guinea, then to Yap and Hong Kong. In 1909 the group again left Hong Kong bound for the German colonies in Micronesia, except for the Marianas, which were considered to be extensively under the cultural influence of the Spanish and the Philippines. Augustin Friedrich Kramer (q.v.) led the expedition, accompanied by his wife, Elisabeth. The expedition, which lasted from 31 July 1909 to 12 March 1910, visited a large number of the islands and atolls of the Carolines and Marshalls.

By 16 April 1910, the Germans were on their way back to Hong Kong and Hamburg where a reception was held on 24 March 1911 in honor of all who took part in the two-year undertaking. The findings of the researchers were published in separate volumes in a series entitled *Ergebnisse der Suedsee-Expedition, 1908–1910.* The series consists of twenty-nine volumes with the first volumes being published in 1913 and the final ones in 1938. The expedition as a whole accomplished its purpose, which was to record in as much detail as possible the cultures of the Pacific peoples under German control before both death and rapidly mounting cultural change had washed away many of the intrinsically interesting and worthwhile indigenous practices. (See Germany in Micronesia; Kramer, Augustin Friedrich)

GERMANY IN MICRONESIA, 1899–1914 The Germans came late to the Pacific and without any territorial ambitions initially. The worldwide trading firm of J. C. Godeffroy and Sohn was the first to establish a regular German presence in Oceania, to carry emigrants to the Australian goldfields, and to trade around the rim of the Pacific with agencies in Chile, North America, Cochin China, and Australia. That was in the 1850s, and Godeffroy came flying the flag, not of Imperial Germany for a German nation-state did not exist until 1870, but of the rich and ancient Hansa city of Hamburg. In 1857 Godeffroys established an agency in Upolu in the Samoan group in order to capture a share of the coconut oil trade.

German penetration of the Pacific grew out of this small beginning.

From Samoa the Godeffroys expanded in all directions: south to Tonga, north to the Marshalls and Carolines in Micronesia, and finally in 1874 to New Britain in the New Guinea islands. Other companies, like that of Eduard Hernsheim based in Micronesia, joined Godeffroys so that by 1879, according to a government memorandum, German firms were exporting from the Pacific some RM6,000,000 in copra, cotton, and shells.

North of New Guinea, the far-flung islands of Micronesia, with the exception of the Marshalls which were annexed in 1885, did not join the German empire until 1899, though German traders had been active there since the 1860s. The Germans, in fact, dominated the copra trade in the area by the mid-1880s, but when Bismarck tried to annex the Carolines and Palau groups in 1885, Spain claimed the islands and the Marianas as part of her old seaborne empire.

The Spanish interlude did not destroy Germany's trade dominance; and when the Micronesian islands were sold to Germany in the wake of the Spanish-American War, this tiny island sphere was in quite a prosperous position. It continued to float along as a reasonably productive appendage of German New Guinea to which it was linked administratively, occasionally devastated by typhoons or disrupted by strikes in the Marshalls or by the major revolt in Pohnpei in 1910, which was put down only by the application of overwhelming German might and severity.

Throughout their thirty years' pre-World War I colonial career, the Germans continually stressed the economic development of the German colonies. The *Deutsches Kolonialblatt* and *Deutsche Kolonialzeitung* devote a major share of their articles from this period to economic development within the colonies and the success that the German firms had there. This economic milieu extended even to the remote islands of the eastern Carolines. At the start of the the German administration there in the fall of 1899, small Japanese companies, called "mini-sosha," were doing a brisk business. But, within two years the Germans deported virtually all the Japanese, leaving the field open for German investment. It is worth noting here that fifteen years later, when the Japanese took control of Micronesia during WWI, they, in turn, ousted all German firms.

When Germany assumed control of the Carolines Islands in July 1899 by means of a purchase agreement with Spain following the Spanish-American war, she had already ruled the Marshall Islands and Nauru for thirteen years through the offices of the *Jaluit Geasellschaft.* When the governor of the New Guinea Protectorate—which included the Bismarck Archipelago, a few of the Solomon Islands, and New Guinea in the ''old protectorate'' in addition to German Micronesia, which was frequently referred to as the *Inselgabiet*—toured the Carolines in October and November 1899, he set up district offices in Pohnpei and Yap. Pohnpei was to serve as the seat of the district government for the eastern Carolines.

From 1900 to 1910, German policy for the eastern Carolines was made by people who cared about the economy above all else and who were convinced that they knew what was best for Micronesia, even to the point of presuming to remove people from their ancestral lands for their own supposed good. This seems pathetic now, but then was regarded with a typically grim Germanic determination, spiced with goodwill and more than a little naivete. All in all, too much faith was placed in the willingness of the Micronesians to adapt, and too little was known about their societies.

Considered as a whole, policy statements found in the annual reports of the district officers on Pohnpei from 1904 to 1909 reveal a growing peace, as well as by a lessening of the power of the chiefs of tenants over their land and crops.

Traffic in guns and ammunition in the eastern Carolines was first secretly and then openly carried on in the middle of the nineteenth century during both the Spanish and the German administration by traders and whalers. This proliferation of weapons created a tense situation for the Germans. They did not want to get involved in a shooting match with the islanders or allow them to shoot one another. To this end, several German warships and escorts of Malayan and Melanesian policemen were sent around to the various groups to expel gunrunners and to purchase guns and cartridges from the islanders.

The *Jaluit Geasellschaft,* which was to administer the Marshalls and Nauru from 1885 through 31 March 1906 by Imperial charter, was granted a monopoly in 1901 for the economic exploitation of the coral atolls in the eastern Carolines.

The main *Jaluit Geasellschaft* station was on Langar Island in Pohnpei Harbor. In fiscal 1904, they built a copra warehouse, a storehouse and a trader's residence on Langar and a large company house, a store, an inn, and a bakery in the colony. By March 1907, the facilities on Langar had expanded to include a cistern, a store, workers' quarters, a garden, a depot for inflammable materials, and a coal shed. Copra was moved around on small four-wheeled carts and iron-tipping wagons that ran along rails running the length of the jetty.

In 1900, the first full year of German administration of the district, *Bizerksamptman* (District Officer) Albert Hahl forecast a gloomy economic picture for the region, citing the limited amount of labor, the distant markets, and high shipping charges. All this would restrict the region to the role of a trading colony. Hahl's gloomy forecast seemed to be borne out by the plight of the coconut plantation owners, most of whom had to exist on the proceeds of their trades. The typhoon of April 1907 further worsened the situation for copra producers there. Furthermore, competition picked up just a year after the typhoon. Japanese traders returned to the eastern Carolines for the first time since the expulsion of the gunrunners in 1901, and the firm of *Murayama Shokai* opened a station on Pohnpei in 1906. A schooner brought in the necessary building materials, and a building was put up in a short time.

Two years later, German companies faced an even more fierce competitor after *Murayama Shokai* merged with the *Nanyo Boeki Hioki Goshi Kaisha* (The Hioki South Seas Trading Company). This merger involved the Pohnpei station, as well as a station on Moen, which had offices, a number of other wood and corrugated iron buildings, and a staff of six men. The new company's name was *Nanyo Boeki Kaisha* (The South Sea Trading Company) (q.v.), which was destined to grow larger and richer than even the *Jaluit Geasellschaft* after World War I.

GIBBONS, JAMES (?–1904) He was a West Indian of mixed blood who became the interpreter to high chief Ibedul of Palau and thereby greatly influenced the direction of foreign contact in Palau. Jumping ship in Palau sometime during the 1860s, Gibbons was valued for his grasp of English and was speedily adopted into the household of the Ibedul, the top-ranking chief of Koror, whom he served until his death. In this position he handled relations between the Ibedul and visiting sea captains. When *HMS Espiegle* came to Palau in August 1883 to intervene in the long-standing dispute between the municipalities of Koror and Melekeok, Gibbons translated the treaty that was drawn up by the British into Palauan.

During the Spanish administration of Palau from 1885 to 1899, Gibbons appears to have held no official position, but when the Germans took control of Palau in 1899, Gibbons was made station supervisor as well as police chief and given a lifetime use of a house and land. It was his responsibility to call the high chiefs into session once a month, especially to promote the cultivation of the coconut palm.

After nearly completing three years of service, Gibbons died on 8 February 1904, and was replaced by a German official. One of his sons, William, served as a policeman during German rule and later became one of the ten top chiefs of Koror. Williams' son, Charlie Gibbons, became a well-known artist and passed away after a long and productive life on 20 July 1988 at the age of ninety-one.

GILBERT AND ELLICE ISLANDS RESIDENT COMMISSIONERS Fifteen men held the post of resident commissioner or governor of this British colony from 1892 to 1978 when the Ellice Islands separated to form Tuvalu:

1893	C. R. Swayne
1895	W. Telfer Campbell
1909	J. Quayle Dickson

1913	E. C. Elliot
1922	H. R. McClure
1926	A. F. Grimble
1933	J. C. Barley
1942	V. Fox-Strangeways
1946	H. E. Maude
1949	W. J. Peel
1952	M. L. Bernacchi
1962	V. J. Andersen
1970	John Field (governor from 1972)
1973	J. H. Smith
1978	R. O. Wallace

GILBERT, ISLANDS, BATTLE OF, 1943 In 1943 the U.S. Joint Chiefs of Staff decided that Admiral Chester Nimitz (q.v.) should advance to Japan through the Central Pacific. They agreed that he should begin his campaign by seizing the Gilbert Islands. The campaign was to be known as Operation Galvanic.

Nimitz chose Vice Admiral Spruance to lead the naval forces and Major General Holland Smith, USMC, to lead the 5th Amphibious Corps on land. The attack was divided in two: A force of 7,000 was sent north to Makin and a force of 18,000 was sent to Tarawa. Both forces were to attack on the same day, 20 November. An enemy garrison of only 800 was found on Makin, and within four days all resistance had been crushed with the loss of 65 Americans. The attack on Tarawa Atoll began with a heavy bombardment of the small island of Betio where there was approximately 5,000 Japanese troops. The men of the 2nd Marine Division met heavy resistance as they struggled ashore. On the night of 22 November, the Japanese, who had been pushed into the interior, made a series of suicidal counterattacks and were cut down. By the next evening the island had been secured. The Americans paid a high price: 1,009 were killed and 2,101 were wounded. The Gilbert Islands were in American hands by 26 November.

GILBERT, THOMAS Gilbert was a British merchant captain. In 1787 Gilbert was given command of the *Charlotte* and sailed for Botany Bay with convicts and soldiers for the new penal settlement as part of the First Fleet. He planned to return to England by way of Macao, and sailed in May 1788 in company with the *Scarborough* commanded by John Marshall (q.v.). They sailed through what would become known as the Gilbert and Marshall Islands. Their charts and sketches provided the first overall picture of these islands. In 1789 Gilbert's account of the voyage was published as *Voyage from New South Wales to Canton.*

GLASS, HENRY (1844–1908) Born in Kentucky, Glass attended the Naval Academy, graduating in 1863. In 1898 he commanded the cruiser *USS Charleston,* which was escorting three troop transports on their way to reinforce Commodore George Dewey's forces in the Philippines. In Hawaii, Glass received orders to take possession of Guam en route to Manila. On 20 June, the convoy reached the island, and after meeting no resistance, Glass accepted the surrender of the Spanish garrison. The American flag was raised over Guam on 21 June. Glass steamed on to the Philippines where he took part in the taking of Manila. He retired from the Navy in 1906 as a rear admiral. The breakwater of Guam's Apra Harbor was named in his honor. (See United States Takes Control of Guam)

GLOBE The Nantucket whaleship *Globe* was the scene of one of the bloodiest mutinies of the whaling period in the Pacific. In January 1824, led by Samuel Comstock, the mutineers killed all the officers and sailed the ship to Mili Atoll in the Marshalls where they tried to set themselves up as rulers over the natives. Disputes soon broke out among the whites and between the Marshallese and the whites. Comstock was killed by other mutineers, and discontented sailors stole the *Globe* and made for South America. Tired of the arrogance and abuse of the whites, the islanders rose up and killed all the remaining mutineers but two: Cyrus Hussey and William Lay, young men who had befriended the Marshallese. These two were rescued two years later. They had been the first Europeans to learn the Marshallese language. In 1828 they published a book (see Bibliography, p. 146) of their experiences. This document, although not scientific, is one of the earliest accounts of Marshallese culture.

GOLDEN HINDE A British warship that sailed into the waters of the western Pacific in the sixteenth century, the *Golden Hinde* made contact with what possibly was Guam but that almost certainly was Palau.

The raising of this land on 30 September 1579 marked the end of 68 days during which the crew saw nothing but air and sea. The lone ship had sailed a course directly across the Pacific, after having laid claim to the west coast of North America in the name of Queen Elizabeth I of England.

The *Golden Hinde* was a 102-foot-long galleon, and her commander was Sir Francis Drake, explorer, colonizer, pirate, and most celebrated English seaman of his time. His interlude in Micronesia, which lasted but a few days, marked a brief stop in a three-year circumnavigation voyage that was to yield $50 million in Spanish booty, enough to pay off all of England's foreign debts.

Captain Drake began the voyage in December 1577 in the same ship that then was called the *Pelican.* After some violent storms around Cape Horn, he rechristened it the *Golden Hinde.* Drake took a wide northern route across the vast Pacific, then came southward and struck land after two months of sailing. He and his crew had a tussle with the islanders in Micronesia, and they departed the islands with a ''backward volley'' to discourage them from following his ship in their outriggers.

Drake went on from Micronesia to the Philippines, across the Indian Ocean, around the Cape of Good Hope, and returned to England on 26 September 1580, and was hailed as the first English circumnavigator. It was one of the great ocean voyages of history.

GREAT MARIANAS TURKEY SHOOT Following the landing of American Marine and Army units on Saipan on 15 June 1944, Japanese fleet elements under the command of Vice Admiral Ozawa Jisaburo steamed toward the Marianas from the southwest to repulse American offensives there. Ozawa had over 400 planes in his command to throw against the

Americans. His pilots, however, were new and poorly trained compared to the American pilots. In the disastrous battle that followed on 18–19 June, the slaughter of Ozawa's force was so rapid and complete that jubilant American airmen dubbed it the "Great Marianas Turkey Shoot." Admiral Ozawa made four thrusts from his carriers against Admiral Marc Mitscher's Carrier Task Force 58. In all, fewer than 100 of the 373 Japanese planes that attacked Task Force 58 managed to return to their carriers. With this shattering defeat at sea Japanese naval air power in the western Pacific evaporated and along with it all hope that the Navy could come to the aid of Saipan.

GUAM The southernmost island in the Marianas chain, Guam lies in approximately 144 degrees east latitude and 13 degrees north longitude, or 1,500 miles east of Manila. The island is within the typhoon belt and is struck by a major storm on the average of once every ten to twelve years.

The island is about thirty miles long and four to eight miles wide. It has an area of approximately 214 square miles. Geologically it is divided into two parts. The southern end is mountainous and of volcanic origin. The highest point, Mount Lamlam, is 1,336 feet above sea level. The northern end consists of a high limestone plateau running between 200 and 600 feet in elevation. The island is surrounded by a coral reef, averaging between 20 to 800 yards in width.

Ferdinand Magellan (q.v.) landed on Guam on 6 March 1521 with three ships, the *Trinidad,* the *Victoria,* and the *Concepcion.* Throughout the sixteenth century, various European navigators visited the island and used it as a source of fresh food and water for their Pacific explorations. Of these, the most important was the Spanish expedition of 1564 headed by Miguel Lopez de Legazpi (q.v.). This expedition claimed Guam for Spain on 26 January 1565, laid the basis for Spanish control of the Philippines, and discovered a reliable return route to North America.

The discovery of this route led to the establishment of direct trade between Manila and Acapulco by means of the yearly voyage of the Manila Galleons (q.v.). On the eastward leg of its voyage, the Galleon stopped at Guam in order to replenish its supplies of food and water. The use of Guam as a source of supplies for the Galleon gave the island a strategic significance that would eventually lead to its conquest by Spain.

Initial contacts between Europeans and Chamorros were marked by a great deal of violence. The inability of the Europeans to understand the reciprocity system of the Chamorros led to charges of thievery, which were punished, often times, by the execution of the Chamorros involved and the burning of their villages. Magellan was so incensed by the Chamorros' behavior that he named the island chain Los Ladrones, or "the islands of thieves." This name continued in use until 1668 when the Jesuit priest Diego Luis de Sanvitores (q.v.), renamed the islands in honor of his patroness, Maria Ana of Austria (q.v.), the wife of Philip IV of Spain.

Throughout the sixteenth and the first two-thirds of the seventeenth century, Spain made no attempt to establish direct control over Guam. This situation changed in 1662 when Father Sanvitores first arrived on Guam. He was so impressed by the Chamorro people that he decided to devote the rest of his life to Christianizing the Marianas. Upon his arrival in the Philippines, he launched a campaign to establish a Jesuit mission on Guam with himself as the superior. After receiving permission, he left the Philippines in 1667 and returned to Guam the following year.

Initially, the mission was successful. This success did not last, however, and in 1670 the Chamorros revolted. The revolt was crushed by the end of the year, but nothing was done to alleviate the tension that had developed between the two cultures. In March 1672 violence erupted once again. Sanvitores was killed shortly thereafter by a high caste Chamorro, Matapang (q.v.), who had forbidden the priest to baptize his daughter.

The death of Sanvitores initiated the Spanish-Chamorro wars of 1672–1695. These consisted of a series of uncoordinated revolts rather than a concerted effort by the Chamorros to oust the Spanish. The lack of unity, the superiority of Spanish weapons, and the inability of the Chamorros to conceive of warfare as something other than a game eventually led to a Spanish victory.

Between 1694 and 1698 Spain resettled the population of the northern Mariana Islands on Guam. The concentration of the population, except for a handful of families on Rota, led to a series of epidemics. These, coupled with military losses, decimated the population. By the end of the wars, the population had been reduced by more than 90 percent.

The Spanish colonial era on Guam consisted of three major periods. During the first period, 1700–1769, Guam was administered by the Jesuit order. The Jesuits established a prosperous mission and continued the Christianization and Hispanization of the population. The second period of Spanish colonial rule, 1769 to 1825, began with the expulsion of the Jesuits from the island and the confiscation of their property by the Spanish state. With the termination of the mission, a secular government under the viceroy of New Spain was established. The resulting arrival of garrison troops, officials, and clerics from Mexico added a North American dimension to Chamorro culture and society. The expulsion of the Jesuits also initiated a period of economic decline that continued virtually unchecked throughout the remaining years of Spanish control.

The collapse of the Spanish Empire in the Western Hemisphere ushered in the final phase of Spanish rule in Guam, from 1825–1898. The administration of the island was shifted from Mexico to the Philippines. This shift, coupled with Spain's decision to utilize the islands as a penal colony for both Filipino and Spanish criminals, intensified the Hispanization of the island and introduced Filipino social and cultural traits into the mainstream of Chamorro culture and society. After the smallpox epidemic of 1856 decimated the population, the Spanish authorities opened Guam to settlement by the Japanese and the Carolinians. At approximately the same time, the northern Mariana Islands were opened to the settlement by these groups and by Chamorros from Guam.

Guam became a United States territory in 1898. In the Treaty of Paris, which ended the Spanish-American War, the island was ceded to the United States and its inhabitants became U.S. nationals. Shortly thereafter, Guam was constituted an unincorporated territory, and administrative authority was delegated to the Department of the Navy. The Navy administered Guam from 1898 to 1950 with the exception of the World War II period, between 1941 to 1944, when the island was occupied by the Japanese.

During the first period of naval rule, 1898–1941, Guam served as a coaling and cable station. The island was viewed as a single naval station and administered accordingly. Life on Guam during this period continued much as it had during the last fifty years of Spanish rule. What development occurred took place primarily in the fields of health and education. In addition, some progress was made in developing a political awareness within the local population.

During World War II when Guam was occupied by the Japanese, the island was incorporated into the Greater East Asian Co-Prosperity Sphere, and administrative control was exercised primarily by the Japanese Navy. The island was retaken by the United States between 21 July and 12 August 1944.

The U.S. Navy resumed sole control of Guam in June 1946. The second period of the naval administration, 1946–1950, had a greater impact on the island than the first. The destruction caused by the war, the establishment of large military bases on the island, and the influx of large numbers of U.S. citizens and Asiatic construction workers began to alter the nature of island society.

In July 1950 the Congress of the United States passed the Organic Act (q.v.) of Guam. This act replaced the naval governor of Guam with an appointed civilian, Carlton Skinner (q.v.), established the twenty-one seat Guam legislature (q.v.), set up a civilian court system, and granted American citizenship to all Chamorros. While the military no longer controlled the island, it continued to play a large role in local affairs.

In 1962 the security clearance (q.v.) required by the military for entrance to Guam was abolished. In the same year, Guam was struck by Typhoon Karen. The abolition of the security clearance and the rehabilitation program undertaken after the storm radically changed the life-style of the island's residents. Commerce and international transportation systems were improved and expanded, media resources were enlarged, the population and immigration continued to increase, and the standard of living of the island's inhabitants rose significantly. To a great extent, these changes have continued into the 1990s.

In 1971 Guam achieved another political milestone with the inauguration of the island's first elected governor, Carlos G. Camacho (q.v.). One year later the island was given a nonvoting delegate in the United States House of Representatives.

Throughout the period since 1700 Chamorro culture was changed and modified. Its basis, however, remained the culture of the pre-Spanish Chamorros. To this base were added layers of Hispanic, Mexican, Filipino, and American cultural traits, which have combined to form the modern Chamorro culture. Since 1970 this culture has come increasingly under attack by the force of changes unleashed after Typhoon Karen. The maintenance and continued development of this culture along with the need to revise the island's political status in light of the growing political sophistication of Guam's population are perhaps the two major issues facing the island in the decade of the 1990s. (See Mariana Islands)

GUAM, APPOINTED CIVILIAN GOVERNORS
Carlton S. Skinner	1949–1953
Ford Q. Elvidge	1953–1956
Richard Barrett Lowe	1956–1959
Joseph Flores	1960–1961
William Daniel	1961–1963
Manuel Flores Leon Guerrero	1963–1969
Carlos Garcia Camacho	1969–1970

GUAM, BANK OF The first financial institution on Guam, the Bank of Guam was established by an executive order issued by Governor W. J. Maxwell in 1915. It was housed in a room in the Governor's Palace in Agana. The bank operated as a branch of the United States Naval Government. It was sold to the Bank of America in 1950 as naval rule on Guam ended. A privately owned bank of the same name was founded in 1972.

GUAM CONGRESS The Guam Congress was an advisory body during the American naval administration of Guam.

The first Guam Congress was convened by Governor Roy C. Smith in 1917. It was an advisory council with no legislative powers. All thirty-four members were appointed by the governor. The membership included certain naval and Marine officers. Since its powers were so limited, several governors ignored the body during the 1920s.

In 1930 Governor Willis W. Bradley (q.v.) dissolved it and established an elected Guam Congress. The first general election in Guam's history took place on 7 March 1931. The new Guam Congress consisted of two houses, an upper house of sixteen members called the House of Council, and a lower house of twenty-seven members named the House of Assembly.

The new Guam Congress also had no legislative power; it was strictly an advisory group. It ceased functioning at the time of the Japanese invasion of the island in 1941.

After the Japanese occupation and a short period of military rule, which followed the American liberation of Guam, naval government was re-established. New elections for the Guam Congress were held in 1946. The next year the Guam Congress was granted certain home-rule powers. This marked the first time since the American occupation in 1898 that a curb was placed on the absolute powers of the naval governor.

The Guam Congress remained in operation until it was replaced by the Guam Legislature (q.v.) in January 1951.

GUAM, CONSTITUTIONAL CONVENTION The United States Congress passed legislation in October 1976 authorizing a constitutional convention. The following year thirty-two delegates were elected to the convention, the purpose of which was to write a constitution for the people of the territory. The resulting document was approved by Congress and President Jimmy Carter, but on 4 August 1979 the constitution was defeated by a five-to-one margin of Guam voters.

GUAM DIKES One of the least-known relics of the Spanish period on Guam is the series of dikes in the heavy jungle growth in the Agana swamp. This large, fertile swamp area, called the Cienaga, challenged several Spanish governors who felt that the area held great potential for growing rice.

Yet, expenditures of large amounts of time, effort, and money never produced the desired results. Later, American governors were equally unsuccessful in their attempts to utilize the swamp area.

Governor Francisco Ramon de Villalobos (q.v.) in 1835 ordered the Agana river to be diverted to run parallel to the sea and through the city of Agana. Water from the stream was used for washing and bathing, but was too brackish for drinking. One of the governor's reports makes reference to only one dike in the Agana swamp. His report related that a swampy valley lay to the east of Sinajana, "where a dike has been made out of rough stone and in the center a wooden bridge to facilitate passage." Governor Felipe Maria de la Corte (q.v.) in 1860 was concerned with people's health and blamed swamp winds for bringing colds and other ailments into Agana. He recommended draining the swamp. By 1885 Governor Olive y Garcia had seen to a partial reclamation of the swamp, and at least two dikes and a system of drainage ditches were noted.

In the American times, several governors concerned themselves with improvements in the swamp, and in 1933 a channel twenty-feet wide and three-feet deep was cut through to the swamp causing the water level to drop and enabling corn and other crops to be planted. Too much maintenance work was required to keep this agricultural effort going, however. The heavy bombardment of World War II did not affect the swamp or the dikes, but they are difficult to locate today without determined guides because the jungle growth is so heavy in the Agana Swamp.

GUAM, ELECTED GOVERNORS

Carlos Garcia Camacho	1971–1974
Ricardo J. Bordallo	1975–1978
Paul M. Calvo	1979–1982
Ricardo J. Bordallo	1983–1986
Joseph Ada	1987–

GUAM, GOVERNORS DURING AMERICAN NAVAL ADMINISTRATION

Governor	Date of Accession
Don Jose Sisto (acting)	June 23, 1898

Don Francisco Portusach (acting)	June 23, 1898
Don Jose Sisto (acting)	January 1, 1899
Don Joaquin Perez (acting)	February 1, 1899
Mr. William Coe (acting)	April 20, 1899
Captain Richard P. Leary	August 7, 1899
Commander Seaton Schroeder	July 19, 1900
Commander W. Swift	August 11, 1901
Commander Seaton Schroeder	November 2, 1901
Commander W. E. Sewell	February 6, 1903
Lt. F. H. Schofield (acting)	January 11, 1904
Lt. Raymond Stone (acting)	January 28, 1904
Commander G. L. Dyer	May 16, 1904
Lt. Luke McNamee (acting)	November 2, 1905
Commander T. M. Potts	March 2, 1906
Lt. Commander Luke McNamee	October 3, 1907
Captain Edward J. Dorn	December 28, 1907
Lt. F. B. Freyer (acting)	November 5, 1910
Captain G. R. Salisbury	January 12, 1911
Captain Robert E. Coontz	April 30, 1912
Commander A. W. Hinds (acting)	September 23, 1913
Captain W. J. Maxwell	March 28, 1914
Lt. Commander W. P. Cronan (acting)	April 29, 1916
Captain Edward Simpson (acting)	May 9, 1916
Captain Roy C. Smith	May 30, 1916
Captain William W. Gilmer	November 15, 1918
Lt. Commander W. A. Hodgman (acting)	November 22, 1919
Captain William W. Gilmer	December 21, 1919
Captain Ivan C. Wettengel	July 7, 1920
Lt. Commander James S. Spore (acting)	October 28, 1921
Captain Adelbert Althouse	February 7, 1922
Commander John P. Miller (acting)	November 8, 1922
Captain Adelbert Althouse	December 14, 1922
Captain H. B. Price	August 4, 1923
Commander A. W. Brown (acting)	August 26, 1924
Captain H. B. Price	October 14, 1924
Captain L. S. Shapely	April 7, 1926
Commander Willis W. Bradley, Jr.	June 11, 1929

Captain Edmund S. Root	May 15, 1931
Captain George A. Alexander	June 21, 1933
Commander Benjamin V. McCandlish	March 27, 1936
Commander James T. Alexander	February 8, 1938
Captain George J. McMillin	April 20, 1940
Rear Admiral Charles A. Pownall	May 30, 1946

GUAM LEGISLATURE The Organic Act (q.v.) of Guam created a unicameral legislature of not more than twenty-one members. The first election was held on 7 November 1950. Members of the Guam Legislature hold office for two years. The legislature has complete law-making powers, although the governor of Guam may veto a bill that has been passed. A two-thirds vote is required to override the veto. (See Guam Congress)

GUAM LEGISLATURE, SPEAKERS

First Legislature	1951–52	Antonio B. Won Pat
Second Legislature	1953–54	Antonio B. Won Pat
Third Legislature	1955–56	Francisco B. Leon Guerrero
Fourth Legislature	1957–58	Antonio B. Won Pat
Fifth Legislature	1959–60	Antonio B. Won Pat
Sixth Legislature	1961–62	Antonio B. Won Pat
Seventh Legislature	1963–64	Antonio B. Won Pat
Eighth Legislature	1965–66	Carlos P. Taitano
Ninth Legislature	1967–68	Joaquin C. Arriola
Tenth Legislature	1969–70	Joaquin C. Arriola
Eleventh Legislature	1971–72	Florencio T. Ramirez
Twelfth Legislature	1973–74	Florencio T. Ramirez
Thirteenth Legislature	1975–76	Joseph F. Ada
Fourteenth Legislature	1977–78	Joseph F. Ada
Fifteenth Legislature	1979–80	Thomas V. C. Tanaka
Sixteenth Legislature	1981–82	Thomas V. C. Tanaka
Seventeenth Legislature	1983–84	Carl T. C. Gutierrez

Eighteenth Legislature	1985–86	Carl T. C. Gutierrez
Nineteenth Legislature	1987–88	Franklin Quitagua
Twentieth Legislature	1989–90	Joe T. San Agustin
Twenty-First Legislature	1991–92	Joe T. San Agustin

GUAM LIBERATION IN WWII The main American objective on Guam was Apra Harbor with its anchorage and airfields. The invading forces landed on beaches five miles apart to the north and south of Apra. On the northern beaches, just southeast of the principal town of Agana, the Third Marine Division faced tough going against Japanese defenders who occupied the high ground all around the beachhead. A Japanese counterattack was beaten off the morning after the initial landings, which were on 21 July 1944. After that, the Marines, well-supported by artillery and naval gunfire, gradually cleared the cliffs and hills.

Five days after the landings, on 26 July, the Japanese delivered a carefully planned counterattack against the Third Marine Division. Small groups of Japanese infiltrated the overextended American lines, while others hurled themselves in bloody frontal attacks against the Marine positions. One battalion of the 9th Marine Regiment absorbed seven such frontal attacks and suffered 50 percent casualties—but the battalion held. In the rear, cooks, clerks, truck drivers, and even hospital patients repulsed the infiltrating Japanese.

To the south, where the First Provisional Marine Brigade, reinforced by the Army's 77th Division, had come ashore against stiff opposition, the Japanese launched a similar attack. They ran headfirst into the corps and division artillery. Pack howitzers were dragged to within 35 yards of the infantry front lines to fire point-blank at the onrushing enemy. ''Arms and legs,'' reported one observer, ''flew like snow.''

The Japanese lost about 3,500 men and up to 95 percent of their officers in the two attacks. Some hard fighting still remained, but on 26 July the defenders had been broken. In the south the First Marine Brigade drove down the Orote Peninsula, which formed the southern end of Apra Harbor. They held the airfields while the 77th Division pushed east and north from the beachhead to join up with the Third Marine Division. Both divisions then swept north, entering Agana on 31 July.

While at Saipan the relations between the Marines and the Army were bad, those on Guam were almost a mutual admiration society. The 77th was an untested division, but it had been exceptionally well-trained and had an aggressive, intelligent commander in the person of Major General Andrew D. Bruce. In the fighting on Guam, the 77th did more than hold their end up.

The 77th and the 3rd Marine Division reached the northern end of the island on 8 August. On 10 August Guam was declared "secure." For the tired soldiers and marines, the conquest of Guam held an interest lacking in other central Pacific battles, for the Japanese had apparently used the island as their major liquor supply dump.

With the recapture of Guam, the Marianas campaign drew to a close. Previously, Saipan and Tinian had been taken, and the other islands were allowed to "die on the vine." Already engineers were busy expanding and improving the island airfields, which shortly thereafter accommodated the new B-29 bombers within range of Japan's poorly defended cities.

GUAM, ORGANIC ACT OF On 1 August 1950 President Harry S Truman signed into law the Organic Act of Guam. This act established civilian government on the island, replacing the United States Naval government. Except for the Japanese occupation from 1941 to 1944, a naval governor had ruled Guam since 1899. An elected twenty-one member legislature and civilian courts were established by the act. Carlton Skinner (q.v.) was appointed first civilian governor.

GUAM, POLITICAL PARTIES Prior to World War II there were no political parties on Guam. In the late 1940s parties began to be organized in anticipation of the passage of Guam's Organic Act (q.v.). The first to do so was called the

Commercial Party comprised mostly of businessmen. To broaden its appeal, the party changed its name to Popular Party in 1950. Eleven years later it became affiliated with the national Democratic Party. The Popular-Democratic Party dominated elections on Guam until the mid-1970s.

Discontented Popular Party members split off to form the Territorial Party in 1956. This party won a majority in the legislature only once, in 1964. It soon dissolved with many of its members joining the newly formed Republican Party. This party was organized in 1966 and won the first gubernatorial election in 1970. In 1974 the Republican Party gained control of the legislature for the first time.

Two short-lived parties on Guam were the Welfare Party (1949–1950) and the Guam Party (1956).

In 1992 the Democratic and Republican were the only parties on Guam, there being eleven Democrats and ten Republicans in the legislature.

GUAM, SPANISH MILITARY COMMANDERS AND GOVERNORS

Military Commanders

Captain Juan de Santa Cruz	June 16, 1668
Captain Juan de Santiago	May 2, 1672
Captain Damian de Esplana	June 16, 1674

Governors

Captain Francisco de Irrisarri y Vinar	June 10, 1676
Captain Juan Antonio de Salas	June 21, 1678
Captain Jose de Quiroga	June 5, 1680
Captain Antonio Saravia	August 1681
Major Damian de Esplana	November 3, 1683
Major Jose de Quiroga	? 1688
Lt. General Damian de Esplana	June ? 1690
Major Jose de Quiroga	August 16, 1694

Major Francisco Madraso y Asiam	September 15, 1700
Major Antonio Villamor y Vadillo	September 1, 1704
Lt. General Juan Antonio Pimentel	September 1, 1709
Captain Luis Antonio Sanchez de Tagle	November 21, 1720
Captain Juan de Ojeda	April 4, 1725
General Manuel Arguelles Valda	September 28, 1725
Major Pedro Laso de la Vega	February 12, 1730
General of the Fleet Francisco Cardenas Pacheco	August 21, 1734
Major Miguel Fernando de Cardenas	April 2, 1740
Captain Domingo Gomez de la Sierra	September 21, 1746
Lt. (Navy) Enrique de Olavide y Michelena	September 8, 1749
General Adres del Barrio y Rabago	November 6, 1756
Lt. (Navy) Jose de Soroa	November 20, 1759
Lt. (Navy) Enrique de Olavide y Michelena	June 9, 1768
Major Mariano Tobias	September 15, 1771
Major Antonio Apodaca	June 15, 1774
Captain Felipe de Cera	June 6, 1776
Lt. Colonel Jose Arlegue y Leon	August 21, 1786
Lt. Colonel Manuel Muro	September 2, 1794
Captain Vicente Blanco	January 12, 1802
Captain Alejandro Parreno	October 18, 1806
Lt. Jose de Medinilla y Pineda	July 26, 1812
Captain Jose Montilla	August 15, 1822
Captain Jose Ganga Herrero	May 15, 1823
Lt. Colonel Jose de Medinilla y Pineda	August 1, 1826
Captain Francisco Ramon de Villalobos	September 26, 1831
Lt. Colonel Jose Casillas Salazar	October 1, 1837
Major Gregorio Santa Maria	October 1, 1843

Treasurer Felix Calvo (acting)	April 7, 1848
Lt. Colonel Pablo Perez	September 8, 1848
Lt. Colonel Felipe Maria de la Corte	May 16, 1855
Lt. Colonel Francisco Moscoso y Lara	January 28, 1866
Colonel Luis de Ybanez y Garcia	August 17, 1871
Lt. Colonel Eduardo Beaumont y Calafat	March 24, 1873
Lt. Colonel Manuel Brabo y Barrera	January 15, 1875
Lt. Colonel Francisco Brochero y Parreno	August 15, 1880
Colonel Angel Pazos Vela-Hildalgo	March 14, 1884
Captain Antonio Borreda	August 4, 1884
Lt. Colonel Francisco Olive y Garcia	November ? 1884
Lt. Colonel Enrique Solano	July 17, 1885
Lt. Colonel Joaquin Vara de Rey	April 20, 1890
Lt. Colonel Luis Santos	August 14, 1891
Lt. Colonel Vincente Gomez Hernandez	August 23, 1892
Lt. of Infantry Juan Godoy (acting)	September 1, 1893
Lt. Colonel Emilio Galisteo Brunenque	October 26, 1893
Lt. Colonel Jacobo Marina	December 24, 1895
Lt. of Infantry Angel Nieto (acting)	February 15, 1897
Lt. Colonel Juan Marina	April 17, 1897

GUAM, UNIVERSITY OF The University of Guam (UOG), founded in 1952 as the Territorial College of Guam, is the major institution of higher learning in Micronesia. It is an American land-grant university, fully accredited by the Western States of Association of Schools and Colleges, with an enrollment of over 3,000. The University of Guam consists of five colleges, a graduate school, and an off-campus center. There are three research units: the Marine

Laboratory, the Water and Energy Research Institute, and the Micronesian Area Research Center.

The University of Guam is governed by a Board of Regents appointed by the governor of Guam on staggered terms. In 1968 the school became a full university with land-grant status. The school plant facility is modern and located on a 10-acre campus in Mangilao on the eastern coast of Guam. (See University of Guam)

GUAM, USS Three American warships have been named *Guam.* The first was a 159-foot-long gunboat launched at Shanghai, China, in 1927. She was assigned to patrol and convoy duty on the Yangtze River. In 1941 her name was changed to the *Wake.* When the war started in December of that year she was captured at Shanghai. The next *Guam* was the second largest cruiser in the American fleet when she entered service in January 1945. She escorted carrier raids in the western Pacific including raids on the Japanese home islands. Placed in reserve in 1947, this *Guam* was scrapped in 1961. The third, and current, ship to bear the name *Guam* is an amphibious assault ship designed to transport 2,000 troops and aircraft. She was launched in 1965.

GUERRERO, MANUEL FLORES LEON (1914–1985) Guerrero was governor of Guam from 1963–1969. Educated in Guam's schools, he began his government career as a messenger for the Naval government in 1930. He was elected to the prewar Guam Congress (q.v.) and the First and Second Guam Legislatures (q.v.). He served in a variety of administrative positions before being appointed governor of Guam. During his administration much of the island's infrastructure was improved, and several urban renewal projects were implemented. Governor Guerrero was instrumental in upgrading the College of Guam to the University of Guam (q.v.). He also oversaw the beginnings of the tourism industry on the island.

H

HASWELL, WILLIAM The first American known to have visited Guam, Haswell was first officer of the barque *Lydia* of

Boston. The *Lydia* was chartered in Manila to take the new governor of the Marianas, Captain Vicente Blanco, to Guam, arriving on 5 January 1802. Haswell spent six weeks on the island. The journal he kept on Guam was later published.

HAYES, WILLIAM HENRY (1829–1877) Born in Cleveland, Ohio, "Bully" Hayes learned his seamanship on the Great Lakes. In about 1850 he began his saltwater career, sailing out of New York City. Three years later he was in Australia. During the 1860s he traded extensively between New Zealand and various Pacific islands. From 1867 to 1875 he used Samoa as his base of operations. He was arrested on Guam in 1875 for aiding in the escape of convicts. He was convicted and spent nine months in a Manila jail. Once released, he resumed trading in Micronesia. He was killed by one of his crew near Jaluit in the Marshalls in 1877.

Hayes acquired a reputation as a swindler, a "South-Seas confidence man," as a fellow trader called him. Many of the dark deeds attributed to him appear to be fiction, however. The writer Louis Becke sailed with Hayes for nine months in 1874. In his short stores, which were published two decades later, he embellished Hayes's exploits, contributing to Hayes being viewed as the last of the South Seas buccaneers. (See Pease, Benjamin)

HOLCOMB, CRAYTON (1838–1885) Captain Crayton Holcomb was a Yankee trader from the state of Connecticut who undertook a series of whaling voyages to the Pacific in the 1850s and 1860s. Lured by bêche-de-mer (q.v.) and shell, Holcomb ventured to Yap in 1874 and established one of the first permanent trading stations on the island. With other traders of the time, including David O'Keefe (q.v.) he helped to establish Yap as a trade center in the late 1870s and thereby exposed the island to later commercial and political influences. As a result of pressure from competitors, however, Holcomb was forced to abandon his own business and leave Yap in 1880. He returned to the island in 1882 and attempted to rebuild his copra (q.v.) trade with borrowed funds, but was frustrated by stiff competition and his own lack of restraint in his dealings with the Yapese.

In 1883 Holcomb was reprimanded by the authorities of a British naval vessel for his part in a white mob's attack on a Yapese village. A year later, in hopes of removing the trade advantage of competing German firms, Holcomb personally presented a petition to the governor of the Philippines signed by himself, his Spanish common-law wife, and some Yapese requesting that Spanish rule be extended to Yap and Palau. This played into the hands of Spanish authorities who were already looking for a pretext to occupy the Caroline islands. But when the formal establishment of Spanish authority in the western Carolines occurred in 1886, Holcomb was not alive to see it.

While on a trading voyage in May 1885, Holcomb was killed by islanders in the St. Mathais group in Melanesia.

J

JAPAN There is a long and interesting history of relations and sensitivities between Japan and Micronesia about which many people on both sides of the Pacific are unaware. As a Pacific area, Micronesia is geographically within the Japanese sphere of influence and traditionally always has been. According to a twelfth-century Japanese literary work, the *Kokin Chomon Shu,* initial Japanese contacts with Micronesians date back at least to A.D. 1171 when some strangers drifted ashore at Okinoshima of Izu, which is the present-day Shizuoka Prefecture. They were possibly from Micronesia, if we can rely on descriptions of their basic features and equipment. If they were indeed Micronesians, these documents might be the oldest record of the Micronesians in the world.

Another major contact of Japan with what is now American Pacific territory occurred in the 1830s when about 20 Japanese drifted ashore at Guam. These people spent the rest of their lives on the island, were assimilated into the local society, and instructed the Chamorros in the planting of rice paddy fields. In the latter half of the nineteenth century, a small number of Japanese were employed by American whalers in the Pacific and had further opportunities for encounters with Micronesians.

In 1884 the Japanese warship *Ryujo* made a call at Kosrae in the Eastern Caroline Islands, and in the same year several Japanese fishermen drifted to the Marshall Islands and were killed by the local people. This caused further Japanese contact with the Marshalls in the way of reprisals and retribution, and marked the beginning of a sustained and growing interest by Japanese in the south seas islands. By the time of the Spanish-American War, the venerable Mori Koben (q.v.) had made his entrance to the south seas and had established himself firmly at Truk, where he would make his fame and fortune and spend the rest of his days as the most celebrated and prominent Japanese settler in Micronesia.

The Spanish-American War brought the Americans and Japanese into near open rivalry in the South Pacific. At Manila Bay, when Commodore George Dewey defeated the Spanish fleet on 1 May 1898, a Japanese squadron stood off watching the encounter in case the Americans did not fare so well. Admiral Togo may have had ideas of his own conquest, and it was commonly known that the Japanese had previously offered aid to the Filipino insurgent leader, Emilio Aguinaldo, in his flight against the Spanish before the Americans even arrived in the islands.

Awareness on the part of the Americans that the Japanese were interested in their Manifest Destiny in the South Pacific caused no little concern and caution. When the Americans captured Guam on 21 June 1898, contingent on the Manila operations of Admiral Dewey, an incident involving a Japanese trading schooner occurred that bespoke the American concern over the Japanese presence in the Marianas. Even though the Spanish were regarded by the American Navy as "a weak and inferior enemy," there were nevertheless round-the-clock combat drills, ordered by Captain Henry Glass (q.v.), for the troops aboard the *USS Charleston,* as they approached Guam. This was because the Americans feared that the Japanese, or possibly the Germans, might attempt to use the faltering Spanish defense of their Pacific empire as an opportunity to seize the islands.

When the *USS Charleston* entered Apra Harbor, the officers and crew noticed a large alien ship anchored there. As the *Charleston* approached, this ship raised the banner of Japan's rising sun. The name *Minatocawa* was written on its stern, and the smaller merchant vessels behind it were also from Japan. For a time Glass's guns remained trained on what appeared to be the unarmed Japanese. Captain Glass boarded the *Minatocawa* and demanded that the skipper explain his presence and inform the Americans about the strength of the Spanish forces on the island. The Japanese captain proved to be cooperative and urged leniency toward the Spanish ashore because they knew nothing, he said, of the war that had been declared between America and Spain.

After the Spanish-American War, the Americans retained Guam and the Philippines as colonies, and Spain sold the Carolines and the rest of the Marianas to Germany for about $6 million. Still, there were tensions between America and Japan and, of course, Germany as well. When World War I broke out in Europe, the Japanese, under secret agreements with the British, chased the Germans out of the Pacific and seized all the German islands north of the equator. At the close of WWI Japan was awarded Micronesia according to the terms of the Treaty of Versailles, but the Americans refused to recognize the Treaty until the Japanese agreed to join the League of Nations and administer Micronesia through a "class C" mandate.

At Guam, matters became increasingly tense for the American Navy, which constantly feared the Japanese presence, which was now completely athwart the ocean routes between Hawaii and the Philippines. An incident known as the Yap Crisis (q.v.) further exacerbated the tensions between the two countries. The Germans had a cable station at Yap in the western Carolines. The Japanese immediately improved the cable station upon their takeover of Yap, and there were reports that the natives of the island were being mistreated. President Woodrow Wilson objected and demanded that Yap be an "international island" because of the communication facilities there. The Japanese finally agreed to this and declared Yap an "open port." All through the mandated period Yap was accessible by all nations. Of course, because of this the Japanese never fully developed Yap, and to this day Yap remains one of the most conservative of the island states in Micronesia, abhorrent or at least discouraging of most outside intrusions and influences.

Some American officialdom expected that when Japan withdrew from the League of Nations in 1933 she would lose her Micronesian colonies, but such did not turn out to be the case. The islands were in a naturally close relationship with Japan and were therefore important in considerations of security and defense.

The horror of the Pacific War, 1941–1945, is still real for many Japanese and Americans, but even this tragedy continued to bind the relationship between Japan and the United States in the case of Micronesia. The bitter fighting was over by late 1944, and almost all Japanese nationals were repatriated by the end of 1946. At that time many families were broken up, and some were not reunited for years afterward. Thus were born the numerous groups that have assisted in the postwar interest in Micronesia in Japan. The best-known of these is the Nan'yo Gunto Kyokai—south seas association—which was formed in 1947 by people who had lived and worked in Micronesia prior to WWII. Many other organizations have been formed in the years since, and they all play a part in increasing the contact and understanding across generations of Japanese and Micronesians.

The Peace Treaty was signed between Japan and the United States in 1951, and after that the relationships in Micronesia began to change dramatically. Some of the prewar Nan'yo Boeki Kaisha (q.v.) managers were contacted by the U.S. Naval authorities and asked to assist with the general commercial supplying of the islands, their expertise being the most well-developed and experienced available. From this time to the present the relationships between the Americans and the Japanese working together in the islands of Micronesia has been enhanced, and this has turned out to be for the benefit of all concerned. (See Nan'yo Boeki Kaisha)

JOHANN C. GODEFFROY UND SOHN Johann C. Godeffroy was a German colonial economic pioneer of Micronesia who established a business with the copra (q.v.) trade throughout Micronesia and other places in the Pacific. The firm of J.C. Godeffroy und Sohn of Hamburg established a factory at Apia, Samoa, in 1856. At first the firm exported coconut oil in casks, but it soon discovered the advantages of shipping unpressed copra. Doing the pressing in Europe yielded a purer oil that was not rancid on arrival, and the residue that resulted from the pressing could be profitably sold for cattle feed.

Beginning in 1865 Godeffroy and Sohn acquired extensive acreage in Samoa for coconut plantations. Others followed suit and plantation-raised coconuts soon furnished most copra. The Kingdom of Tonga, which at that time was politically more stable than Samoa, soon became the company's main supplier. In 1869 Godeffroy entered into an agreement with the Wesleyan Mission, which gave the German firm virtual monopoly of Tonga's export trade.

By the 1870s Godeffroy's agents were scattered all across the Pacific from Tahiti to Guam and the northern Marianas. But their economic bright star did not last. Godeffroy and Sohn collapsed in 1879 due to some unsuccessful Pacific island mining speculation it had become involved with and also from domestic difficulties at home in Germany as a result of the Franco-Prussian War.

Godeffroy and Sohn's holdings and role in the economic life of the islands was then taken over by other firms, but their memory and contributions will always remain as important ones for the Pacific. (See Germany; Kubary, Johann Stanislaus)

JOHNSTON, AGUEDA I. (1892–1977) Born in Agana, Johnston attended grammar school there, continuing her education through correspondence courses. She began teaching when she was fifteen years old. She became a principal in 1925, later opening Guam's first junior high school, Seaton Schroeder School, and serving as its principal until 1936. In that year she became the first principal of George Washington High School and the Teacher's Institute, posts that she held for ten years. In 1946 she became assistant superintendent of education, a position she held until her retirement in 1955. Johnston also was a member of Guam's Board of

Education from 1965–1973. Her accomplishments led to her being listed in *Who's Who in America* and the *World Who's Who of Women.*

K

KAVA See Sakau

KIRIBATI, REPUBLIC OF Kiribati (pronounced "kiribass") consists of three groups of islands: the Gilbert, Phoenix, and Line islands. There are thirty-three islands in all scattered over 2 million square miles of ocean astride the equator. The nearest neighbors are Nauru to the west and Tuvalu to the south. The population in 1985 was 63,883.

The British sailors Byron (in 1765), Thomas Gilbert (1788) (q.v.), and John Marshall (1788) (q.v.) discovered several of the islands, although they may have been sighted by Spanish explorers in the sixteenth century. The rest of the islands were discovered by Americans and Europeans between 1798 and 1826. The name Gilbert Islands came into use in the 1820s. During the middle nineteenth century the islands were a favorite ground for the whaling (q.v.) fleets. Hiram Bingham of the American Board of Commissioners for Foreign Missions (q.v.) established a mission on Abiang in 1857.

The Gilberts and nearby Ellice Islands were made into a British protectorate in 1892. In 1916 they became a crown colony. During 1942–1943 the islands were invaded by the Japanese. Some of the fiercest fighting of World War II took place on Tarawa in 1943 as the Americans seized the island from the Japanese.

In 1976 the Ellice Islands separated to form Tuvalu, an independent country. The inhabitants of the Ellice Islands are Polynesian. In 1977 the Gilberts, Line, and Phoenix islands became self-governing, and in 1978 they emerged as the independent republic of Kiribati. ("Kiribass" is the closest sound to the world "Gilberts" that the islanders can manage in their indigenous language.)

Kiribati has a unicameral thirty-nine-member legislature whose members serve for four-year terms. The head of state is a popularly elected president, who governs with the assistance of a vice president and Cabinet. Island Councils constitute the local government.

The economy is based on fishing and copra (q.v.). Tourism (q.v.) is a small but growing industry.

KOTZEBUE, OTTO VON (1787–1846) A graduate of the Russian Naval Cadet School, Kotzebue, an ethnic German from Estonia, led two Russian scientific expeditions to the Pacific. On his first voyage, from 1815–1818, he was instructed to search for the Northeast Passage—the waterway that supposedly connected the Bering Sea with the Atlantic. In addition, he explored many of the island groups in the Pacific, including the Marshalls where he spent almost three months in early 1817. This was the first prolonged contact between Europeans and Marshallese. Kotzebue bestowed Russian names on many of the atolls and produced intricate maps of parts of the archipelago. He kept detailed accounts of his dealings with the Marshallese and recorded significant details of the islanders' way of life. On his second voyage, from 1823–1826, he revisited the Marshalls, adding to the information collected on his first voyage. The journals of both voyages were published in several languages.

KRAMER, AUGUSTIN FRIEDRICH (1865–1941) German ethnologist and explorer of the South Pacific, Kramer studied medicine in Tubingen and Berlin and natural science in Kiel. In 1889 he joined the imperial navy and soon after began a series of expeditions to the German protectorates in the South Pacific where he collected abundant anthropological data. Kramer's first cruise (1893–1895) on the *S.M.S. Bussard* included a twelve-month stay in Samoa. Kramer visited the islands once again, from 1897–1899, during which time he was involved in various German intrigues among the rival Samoan chiefs. In 1906 Kramer traveled as an anthropologist aboard the *S.M.S. Planet* in the Atlantic and Indian Oceans and to the Bismarck Archipelago. He also visited Truk, Yap, and Palau in the Carolines in 1906–1907 and led a German naval expedition to New Mecklenburg. Kramer commanded the second phase of the German South Sea Expedition (q.v.)

to the Caroline and Marshall islands in 1909–1910, gathering much anthropological, zoological and geological, and geographical information along the way. Kramer later became the scientific director of the Linder-Museum in Stuttgart and also published many scholarly works, including *Die Samao-Inseln (1902–1903),* based on the ethnographical and biological material accumulated during his South Seas travel.

KUBARY, JOHANN STANISLAUS (1846–1896) A German-Polish ethnographer and naturalist, Kubary was the first European to seriously investigate the origins and usage of the traditional Palauan money *udoud* (q.v.) and report on it in the late nineteenth century.

Kubary was born in Warsaw, Poland, in 1846 of a German mother and Hungarian father. His father died when he was very young and so he was reared in the home of his Polish stepfather. Following a troubled childhood, Kubary began to study medicine at age seventeen. He became involved in agitation for Polish independence and, after several bouts with authorities, fled to Hamburg, Germany.

Through the good offices of a museum patron named J.D.S. Schmeltz, he met Johann C. Godeffroy (q.v.), a prominent and wealthy shipper whose Pacific offices were in Samoa. Godeffroy, who had a passion for ethnography and artifact collecting, employed Kubary as a collector for his Hamburg Museum as well as an amasser of information for his *Journal des Museum Godeffroy.*

From 1870 to 1874 Kubary did extensive fieldwork throughout Micronesia. Kubary discusses Palauan traditional money at length in two separate Godeffroy journal articles. One is ''Dei Palau-Inseln in der Suedsee,'' where Palauan money is discussed under the heading ''Das Palau-Geld.'' Later, in a collection of five articles entitled ''Ethnographische Beitrage zur Kenntnis des Karolinen Archipels,'' the lead article ''Ueber das einheimische Geld auf der Insel Yap und auf den Palau-Inseln'' (concerning the indigenous money of the Island of Yap in the Palau Islands), he treats Palauan money at greater length.

In 1874, aboard a homeward bound Godeffroy ship, Kubary was shipwrecked near Jaluit in the Marshall Islands with reportedly 100 barrels of carefully packed specimens. He arrived in Hamburg with only a small portion of the irreplaceable collection.

In 1875 Kubary went to the Eastern Carolines and established himself at Pohnpei where he purchased land and planted botanical gardens. He married a Pohnpeian woman who bore him a son and a daughter and who was his faithful companion in his worldwide wanderings.

Following the Franco-Prussian War in 1879, Godeffroy was ruined and both Kubary and the museum were casualties. After his abandonment by Godeffroy, Kubary went to Japan to try to start a museum in Tokyo, but this effort failed. He again tried through Leiden, but this also failed.

Discouraged, depressed, and bankrupt, Kubary withdrew from scientific work and took employment as an interpreter on a German warship cruising the Pacific. At New Guinea he and his family disembarked, and he got a job as a shopkeeper for a German trading company.

Finally, in 1895, Kubary returned to Pohnpei with his family and again faced dejection and tragedy. His only son died of a fever and was buried in his botanical gardens. These were subsequently destroyed by fire, which resulted from a Spanish naval bombardment against some Pohnpeian rebels. In 1896 Kubary took his own life at Pohnpei.

In all, Kubary spent twenty-six years in the Pacific, most of them in Micronesia. His writings on Palauan money and on many other ethnographic and historical matters remain a basis for understanding late nineteenth-century Micronesia.

KWAJALEIN, BATTLE OF, 1944 American victories at Tarawa and Makin in November 1943 encouraged Admiral Chester W. Nimitz (q.v.) to bypass the eastern Marshall Islands and seize Kwajalein Atoll in the west. The islands of Roi and Namur in the northern part of the atoll were assigned to the 4th Marine Division, while the more heavily defended Kwajalein Island in the south of the atoll was given to the Army 7th Infantry Division as an objective. After capturing small nearby islands beforehand, troops landed on Kwajalein on 1 February. Following five days of determined enemy resistance, Kwajalein fell on 6 February, and the atoll was declared secure. The Americans lost only 373 men in the battle.

L

LANGUAGE Micronesians speak Austronesian languages that are different from those of Polynesia. Ten major languages are spoken: Chamorro and Palauan are classified as Indonesian, while Yapese, Ulithian, Chukese, Pohnpeian, Koraean, Nauruan, Gilbertese, and Marshallese are Micronesian.

LATTE STONES *Latte* stones, called *Taga stones* in the northern Marianas, are megalithic columns and capitals that were ostensibly made to support houses. They are commonly five- to six-feet high, with some smaller. Yet, the *latte* of the "House of Taga," a prehistoric site on Tinian in the Northern Marianas, measure sixteen feet in height. At Rota (Luta) there is a *latte* quarry with partially hewn stones present. *Latte* were built from around A.D. 1000 to 1650.

LEARY, RICHARD P. (?–1901) First American governor of Guam, who served from 1899–1900. Leary graduated from the Naval Academy in 1860. He participated in the U.S. Civil War and the Samoan revolution of 1888. His expulsion of the Spanish priests from Guam led to protests in the American press. Most of the details of governing Guam he left to his aide, Lt. William Safford (q.v.).

LEE BOO (1764–1784) Also Lebu, Leeboo, Leebu. He was a young Palauan, nineteen or twenty years old, who accompanied Captain Henry Wilson from his shipwreck site at Ulong, Palau, in 1783 to Macao, and then to England.

Lee Boo might have been the son of a Yapese mother and Palauan father. His mother might have lived at Peleliu island in Palau. The youth was brought to Koror and adopted by the Ibedul, the highest chief of Koror.

Captain Henry Wilson was shipwrecked in the British East India Company packet *Antelope* on 10 August 1783, and came ashore at Ulong Island neaer Koror. He and his crew were befriended by the Ibedul, and together they constructed another ship of a mixture of local and British design. On 12 November 1783, the British departed Palau and left behind one crewman, Madan Blanchard. (q.v.) In exchange, the Ibedul sent his adopted son, Lee Boo, with Wilson to be educated in the English ways and then to return to Palau.

In their new ship, the *Orolong* (Ulong, named for the island they were shipwrecked upon), they sailed to Macao and then to Canton, China, and Portsmouth, England, on the *Morse*. In England, Lee Boo lived with Wilson and his family in their home at Rotherhithe, London, where he became well-liked and popular in the community. He contracted smallpox and died on 27 December 1784, and was buried in the Wilson plot at St. Mary's church in Rotherhithe, where he rests today.

A best-selling book, *An Account of the Pelew Islands,* by George Keate was published from Wilson's notes in 1785 and became a best-seller throughout Great Britain and Europe with editions in French and German.

LEGAZPI, MIGUEL LOPEX DE (b. ca. 1510–1572) Born in Spain about 1510, Legazpi went to New Spain (Mexico) in 1545. In 1564 he led an expedition of four ships, which were sent to the Philippines to claim those islands for Spain. On the voyage he discovered Mejit, Ailuk, Jemo, and Wotho in the Marshalls. Legazpi went ashore at Guam on 26 January 1565 and claimed the Marianas (then called the Ladrones) for Spain. The expedition sailed on to the Philippines. On his return to Acapulco, Legazpi crossed the Pacific on a northern route, around forty degrees north latitude. He also carried a cargo of Asian goods. This was the start of the galleon trade. (See Manila Galleons; *San Pablo*)

LELU RUINS One of the most impressive yet least-known archaeological sites in the Pacific are the Lelu ruins on Kosrae. Lelu flourished as the feudal capital of Kosrae from A.D. 1400 to A.D. 1800; the kings and high chiefs had their residences there. The city covered the entire plain area of Lelu and included 100 walled compounds. Warriors from

Lelu invaded Pohnpei and conquered Nan Madol. The ruins consist of crisscrossed basalt blocks, and there are the remnants of the network of canals that brought canoe traffic through the city. Some of the walls are six meters high.

LEON GUERRERO, FRANCISCO BAZA (1898–1974) Leon Guerrero was a Guam educator, politician, and farmer. Born and educated on Guam, he was a teacher before joining the Department of Agriculture in 1918. During these years he studied law and was admitted to the Guam bar. He was a member of the prewar Guam Congress (q.v.) and the Third Guam Legislature (q.v.). A consistent advocate of a greater measure of self-government for the people of Guam, he was often referred to as "Mr. Organic Act." He traveled with B. J. Bordallo (q.v.) to Washington, D.C., in 1936 in their unsuccessful effort to have United States citizenship and civil rights extended to the people of Guam. In 1950 he was back in Washington to testify in favor of the bill that would eventually become the Organic Act (q.v.) of Guam.

LEONORA The *Leonora* was one of the most famous sailing ships in Micronesia during the last century. It was mastered by the notorious ship captain, adventurer, blackbirder, and scoundrel Bully Hayes. (q.v.) The *Leonora* was formerly known as the *Pioneer,* but Hayes took it over in 1872, had it painted white, and renamed it the *Leonora* after one of his twin daughters. The *Leonora* was a brigantine and looked like a yacht. Her master cabin contained a fine gun collection, and she also carried four cannons.

Captain Bully Hayes was an unsavory character who had copra stations scattered around the Caroline and Marshall islands and sold his copra to the German firm of Johann C. Godeffroy und Sohn (q.v.) in Apia, Samoa. On 15 March 1874, the *Leonora* was lying at anchor at Utwe Harbor at Kosrae when a sudden tropical storm caused her to drag anchor and pile into a reef where she was pounded and sunk by the high surf.

The sinking of the *Leonora* led to tales of buried treasure at Kosrae. Authors Frank Clune and Louis Becke wrote that the ship's boats and most of the cargo, including some gold, were removed before the ship sank. Captain Hayes escaped from Kosrae in one of the *Leonora*'s boats to avoid a British warship that was searching for him. He intended to return to Kosrae but was killed by one of the crew on his next ship.

In November 1964, an American contract schoolteacher Harvey Segal, and a Kosraean fisherman Alik Luke, found the wreck of the *Leonora* in nine fathoms of water. This was verified by Scripps Oceanographic Laboratory divers in 1968. Some artifacts of the *Leonora* may be seen today in the museum at Kolonia, Pohnpei, and also at the Scripps Oceanographic Laboratory in La Jolla, California.

LIFE-STYLE CHANGES One characteristic of Pacific history has been rapid social changes following contact between white people and islanders. Often this contact was abrupt, sometimes harsh. In recent decades especially, exchange between traditionally distinct societies has increased dramatically, and characteristics of life in the twentieth century have jointly influenced patterns of human behavior with regard to health. Nowhere is this more apparent than in societies of relatively recent exposure to the modern world, and it is not likely that the sequence can be reversed. This acculturation, or mixing of cultures, resulted in new roles and life-style that were not part of earlier Pacific patterns. Such changes for traditional authorities, families, and individuals have resulted in new stress patterns, and syndromes, for contemporary Oceania.

Changes of life-style from rural subsistence to town and city living, the money economy, modern technology and work, and different consumption patterns further promote the appearance of new stress-related patterns of behavior. These can be made even worse from diet deficiencies such as undernutrition, protein-calorie malnutrition, and high intake of starches, sugar, and salt. Such syndromes also are expressed as psychosomatic maladies, for example, obesity, diabetes, hypertension, and heart disease. Significant also are increased mental health problems, especially among urban residents, abuse of alcohol and drugs, and automobile accidents.

These stress-related behavior patterns or syndromes are part of the changing Pacific world and call for broad and practical attention. Stress is a necessary part of life and can be productive if it leads to learning and growth. The challenge is how to manage these new stress-related problems.

LOGAN, ROBERT W. (1852–1887) A prominent Protestant missionary in Truk (Chuuk) in the Eastern Caroline Islands, Logan was ordained in 1870 and joined the Pohnpei mission in 1874. There he learned the Mortlockese dialect and visited the Mortlocks with fellow missionary Albert Sturges (q.v.) in 1877. Subsequently he was stationed in Oneop Island in 1879. He translated the Bible and a number of other religious books into Mortlockese. He visited the United States and then returned to Truk with his wife to establish a mission on Moen Island in 1884. Reverend Logan died of a fever in Truk in 1887. (See American Board of Commissioners for Foreign Missions; Boston Mission Schools; Doane, Edward T.; *Morning Star;* Sturges, Albert)

LUTKE, FEDOR PETROVICH (1797–1882) A Russian explorer who sailed around the world with V. M. Golovnin in the sloop *Kamchatka* in 1817–1819, Lutke led his own expedition to the Pacific in 1826–1829. His main work was in the Carolines in late 1827 and 1828. After his return to Russia he published an account of his voyage, which included a detailed report and charts of the Carolines. He is credited with discovering the island of Eauripik in the western part of the group.

M

MAGELLAN, FERDINAND (1480–1521) Also Fernando Magellanes. Magellan was the Portuguese mariner in command of the first expedition to circumnavigate the globe and to discover the Mariana Islands in the process. With five ships and over 200 crewmen and officers, Magellan left Spain on 20 September 1519, and sailed for the Canary Islands in the Atlantic. He traveled down the east coast of South America visiting every bay and estuary.

On 2 April 1520, he vigorously put down a mutiny and imprisoned, marooned, or executed some mutineers. On 3 May

1520, one of his ships, the *Santiago* was wrecked in a storm, but the crew and most of the provisions were saved. On 21 October 1520, Esteban Gomez, captain of the ship the *San Antonio* deserted and returned to Spain with the crew. On 28 November 1520, Magellan entered the Pacific Ocean after passing through the straits that now bear his name with a fleet of three remaining ships, the *Trinidad,* the *Concepcion,* and the *Victoria.* After two and a half months, they sighted two small uninhabited islands, which have since been identified as Pukapuka and Caroline of the Tuamotu. Magellan was unable to land, but the crew did catch some fish.

No other land was sighted until 6 March 1521, when they sighted the Marianas and landed at Guam on the northwest coast. The crews were weak and sick and twenty-nine died of various ailments with another thirty very ill. They stayed three days to reprovision. After Chamorro natives took a small skiff that was trailing behind one of the ships, Magellan went ashore, burned a village, and killed an undetermined number of people. Thus Magellan became the first European to order the killing of Pacific islanders.

On 9 March, he departed Guam for the Philippines where he later encountered and became involved in local native rivalries and was killed on 27 April 1521; his body was not recovered. The voyage continued without the badly damaged *Concepcion,* which had to be scuttled. The *Trinidad,* under the command of Jaoa Lopez Caravalho, headed back into the Pacific homebound, but was later captured and interned by the Portuguese. The *Victoria,* under the command of Sebastian del Cano (also Elcano), pressed onward across the Indian Ocean toward the Cape of Good Hope. They encountered storms and fears of the Portuguese during the rest of their nine-month, 11,000-mile voyage, but they returned home to Spain in August 1522. Only eighteen of the original crew remained, and three Pacific islanders arrived in Spain with them. (See Pigafetta, Antonio)

MAILO, PETRUS (?–1969) A Chuukese (Trukese) elected political leader, Mailo was also a traditional leader of Chuuk who was born to a chiefly clan of Moen Island. He became the most important political figure in Truk during the early period of American administration following World War II and was known and respected throughout Micronesia. Mailo acquired the traditional knowledge of *itang* (which is an esoteric powerful military astuteness). He effectively combined the authority of traditional and elected political office.

Mailo was educated at a Protestant elementary school during the German colonial period. He was appointed adviser on island affairs for the Japanese civil and military governments and he coordinated the relocation of Moen's people during the war. When the American government was formed in 1947, he became magistrate and chief of Moen municipality. He was elected mayor when Moen was chartered in 1957 and held the post until his death. He served in the Truk district congress from 1957 until 1962.

Chief Petrus, as he was locally known, was elected to the House of Representatives of the first Congress of Micronesia (q.v.) and served as Vice Speaker until his resignation in 1968. Petrus traveled to Japan and the United States on leadership tours but is remembered best for his efforts to serve his people of Truk in both public and private capacities. He was responsible for establishing savings institutions based on traditional forms of contribution and became president of the largest trading company with local shareholders. He arbitrated disputes between different islands, convened magistrate conferences, and argued that the Trukese people should combine the good things of traditional and Western culture.

MAKIN, RAID ON, 1942 Makin Atoll was reported to be the Japanese stronghold in the Gilberts. To secure intelligence about Japanese installations, strength, and inclination to fight, Admiral Chester Nimitz (q.v.) determined to conduct a reconnaissance in force using one of his newly organized Marine Raider Battalions. Two submarines carried the 2nd Raider Battalion commanded by Lt. Colonel Evans Carlson to the Gilberts from Honolulu. Carlson's executive officer was Major James Roosevelt, the President's son. The raid took place on 17 August. The Americans suffered eighteen casualties, while there were 200 Japanese killed. The raid on Makin made headlines in the American press.

MANILA GALLEONS These were large Spanish ships that carried cargo across the Pacific from Manila in the Philippine Islands to Acapulco on the west coast of modern-day Mexico and then back to Manila during the period from 1565–1815. Exotic goods from the Orient, such as Chinese silk, cotton from India, tapestries, gold, gems, and spices, were shipped in the galleons to Mexico. Eventually most of these goods reached Europe. On the return trip, the ships carried Mexican and Peruvian silver. At its peak the galleon trade was one of the major avenues of trade between China and Europe.

Guam was a regular stop on the vessels' return voyage to Manila. The funds needed for the maintenance of the Marianas colony were brought by the annual galleon. In addition, missionaries, soldiers, mail, and official correspondence were delivered to the islands. English privateers hunted the galleons, with little success, starting with Drake in 1579. Thomas Cavendish, Woodes Rogers (q.v.), George Anson (q.v.), and William Dampier (q.v.) followed, all visiting the Micronesian waters at some time while following the galleon route. (See Legazpi; *San Geronimo; San Pablo*)

MARIANA ISLANDS Situated between 13 and 20 degrees north latitude and 140 degrees east longitude, the Marianas are volcanic and coral islands. Guam (q.v.) is the largest and southernmost, and Farallon de Pajaros is the northernmost. There are twenty-two islands in all, with fifteen being the main ones and only five being seriously occupied with people. Their total land area is some 309 square miles. Guam, Saipan, Tinian, Rota, and Pagan are populated; the 1990 population was about 176,497.

The Marianas were discovered by Magellan (q.v.) in 1521 during his circumnavigation. They were colonized in 1668 by the Spanish Jesuit Fray Diego Luis de San Vitores (q.v.). Magellan named them "Los Ladrones," the "thieves islands," and San Vitores renamed them the Marianas in honor of Queen Mariana of Spain.

A rich marine fauna exists in the open seas, reefs, lagoons, and shore areas. The gecko and fruit bat are indigenous, and the Spanish introduced deer, carabao, and a number of plants.

There are also dogs, cats, and pigs running wild in the Marianas.

When the Spanish arrived they found native people, called Chamorros (q.v.), living in the Marianas; these natives have now mixed with other races and peoples but survive with the same name of Chamorros. They were peaceful people living in a matrilineal society. In 1898 the United States captured Guam from Spain; the remaining islands were sold to Germany by Spain for about $5 million. In 1914 Japan seized the Marianas, except Guam, from Germany and occupied Guam in 1941 at the outbreak of World War II. After a series of bloody battles, the United States recaptured Guam and the rest of the Marianas in 1944.

By an Organic Act (q.v.) in 1950 the people of Guam became U.S. citizens and Guam became an unincorporated territory of the United States. The northern Marianas became a United Nations trusteeship with the U.S. as administrator. In 1978 the Northern Marianas became a commonwealth of the U.S. (See Commonwealth of the Northern Mariana Islands)

MARIANA, QUEEN (1634–1696) Mariana was the daughter of the Austrian Hapsburg Emperor Ferdinand III and his Spanish-born Hapsburg wife Maria Ana. In 1649, she married King Philip IV of Spain. Upon the death of her husband in 1665, she became Queen Regent of Spain. Influenced by Jesuits at court, she supported their missionary work, including the mission of Diego Luis de San Vitores (q.v.) to Guam. San Vitores named the Mariana Islands after her because of her assistance.

MARSHALL, JOHN Marshall was a British merchant captain. In 1787 he was given command of the *Scarborough* and sailed for Botany Bay with convicts and soldiers for the new penal settlement as part of the First Fleet. In May 1788 Marshall sailed for Canton accompanied by the *Charlotte* commanded by Thomas Gilbert (q.v.). They sailed through what would become known as the Gilbert and Marshall islands. Their sketches and charts provided the first overall picture of these islands. Little is known of Marshall's later life.

MARSHALL ISLANDS The Republic of the Marshall Islands consists of two groups of islands, the Ratak (sunrise) chain and the Ralik (sunset) chain, which comprise thirty-one atolls. The islands lie about 2,000 miles southwest of Hawaii and about 1,300 miles southeast of Guam. In 1988 the population was 43,355.

The Marshalls were discovered by the Spaniard Alvaro de Saavedra Ceron (q.v.) in 1529. The British captain John Marshall (q.v.) partially explored them in 1788 and gave them his name. Russian expeditions under Krusenstern (in 1803) and Otto von Kotzebue (q.v.) (in 1815 and 1823) did much mapping. German trading companies were active from the 1850s onward. Spanish sovereignty was recognized over the islands in 1886 by the Papal Bull of Pope Leo XIII, which also gave Germany trading rights there. Spain sold the group to Germany in 1899 after the Spanish-American War. In 1914 Japan occupied the Marshalls and received a League of Nations mandate to administer the islands in 1920. After the capture of the Marshalls by American forces in 1944, most of the Japanese settlers were repatriated. In 1947 the United Nations established the Trust Territory of the Pacific Islands (q.v.) with the Marshalls being administered by the United States along with the Carolines and the northern Marianas. From 1965 on, there was increasing demand for local autonomy. In that year the Congress of Micronesia was (q.v.) formed, and in 1967 a commission to examine the future political status of the islands was established. In 1977 President Jimmy Carter announced that his administration intended to terminate the trusteeship agreement. The Marshall Islands drafted its own constitution, which came into effect in 1979. The United States signed the Compact of Free Association with the Marshalls in 1982. Under the compact, the Marshalls would manage its internal and foreign affairs, while the United States would be responsible for defense and security. In addition, the United States was to retain its military bases for at least fifteen years and was to provide annual aid of $30 million. The compact went into effect in October 1986.

The constitution of the Marshall Islands provides for a parliamentary form of government. The thirty-three member legislative body, the Nitijela, elects a president from among its own members. The Nitijela is advised by the House of Iroiji, which is comprised of traditional leaders. Local governmental bodies are the municipalities and villages. Amata Kabua was elected president of the Republic of the Marshall Islands in 1986. He is the only person to hold that office.

MARTINEZ, PEDRO PANGELIAN (1892–1967) Born on Guam, Martinez attended local schools and St. Mary's College (Raleigh, North Carolina) and Valparaiso University (Valparaiso, Indiana). He returned to Guam in 1913 employed by the Navy. He went into private business in 1921, starting a variety of successful companies, including an ice and cold storage plant, an automobile agency, and a construction firm. Martinez was also active in public service as an associate justice of the Court of Appeals and a member of the Board of Pardons. After the devastation of the second World War, he rebuilt his businesses and was active in civic organizations and the Catholic church.

MASTERS, SAMUEL J. (1801–1882) Masters was the first and only U.S. Consul stationed at Guam during the Spanish administration. He was born in 1801 in Schaghticoke, Rensselaer County, New York. His father had served in both the New York State Legislature and the U.S. Congress and was an important leader in the Democratic Party of his time. Young Masters worked for twenty years as a captain aboard commercial vessels trading with the West Indies before being appointed U.S. Merchant-Consul to British Guyana by President James K. Polk. In 1853 Captain Masters was appointed police magistrate in Lahaina, Maui, Hawaii, and then in November 1854, he arrived at Guam under appointment from Secretary of State William D. Marcy in the administration of President Franklin Pierce.

The Spanish didn't want him to come and in fact never officially recognized his presence; one reason for this may have been that the U.S. at the time was investigating complaints against the Spanish for mistreatment of American citizens on Guam. Captain Masters was part of that investigation.

The investigation involved the visit of an American warship to Guam, the *USS Vandalia,* and this was both embarrassing and intimidating to the Spanish authorities. After the ship left, Captain Masters was all but completely ignored by the Spanish, and when public works refused to fix his living quarters after a severe typhoon had blown the roof off, Masters left in frustration. (See Corte, Felipe de la)

MATAPANG (?–1680) Matapang was the Chamorro leader of the village of Tumon on the west coast of Guam. He himself had been baptized by the Jesuit missionary Diego Luis de San Vitores (q.v.), but when the priest baptized his daughter Matapang objected. In April 1672, Matapang and an accomplice murdered San Vitores. Eight years later, Governor Quiroga led a military expedition to Rota in search of a number of Chamorro leaders, including Matapang. In an attempt to win favor with the Spaniards, the Chamorros decided to sacrifice Matapang. He was attacked and severely wounded. He died in a canoe on his way to Guam.

McMILLIN, GEORGE J. (1889–1984) McMillin was governor of Guam from 1940–1941. Born in Ohio he attended schools there and later attended the Naval Academy from which he graduated in 1911. He served in various ships in both the Atlantic and Pacific fleets and was on the staff of the Naval War College from 1936–1938. He assumed his duties as governor of Guam on 20 April 1940, and was still in office when the Japanese invaded the island on 10 December 1941. He surrendered the island after only token resistance. McMillin spent the war years in prison camps. He returned to active duty after the war, retiring in June 1949.

MENDANA, ALVARO (ca. 1541–1595) Dispatched from Peru in 1567 on a mission to find the supposedly gold-rich *Terra Australis,* the Spaniard Mendana discovered the Solomon Islands instead. Returning home the following year, he discovered Namu Atoll in the Marshalls.

MENTOR The first Americans ever to visit Palau were most likely the crewmen of the American whaleship *Mentor.* In May

1832, the *Mentor,* coming from the Celebes and headed for Guam, struck the northern Palau reefs and sank quickly. Captain Edward Barnard and his twenty-one crewmen made it to a shoal and waited until morning when they were then rescued by the curious Palauans and eventually taken to the municipality of Ngerchelong, where Palauans flocked around them to gaze interestedly.

It was only about 50 years since the visit of British Captain Wilson in the *Antelope,* and these northern Palauans wanted, apparently, to make friends with the Americans similarily as the Koror people had made friends with the British. They assisted the Americans in constructing a curious canoe of mixed Palauan and American whaleboat design. In this craft, on 27 October 1832, ten Americans and three Palauans set sail.

The voyage was a disaster. They were swamped in a storm and finally made it ashore at Tobi Island on 6 December where the survivors were made captives by the islanders there. For more than two years they were made to work as slaves for the Tobians. They were given little food and worked very hard. In addition to this, they were tattooed over large parts of their bodies, and this caused further weakness to their already emaciated conditions.

On 27 November 1834, the British barque *Britannia* rescued the two surviving Americans, Horace Holden and Benjamin Knute. When they returned to America, Holden wrote a chronicle of their adventures, and it has proved to be a valuable source of information on the Palauan culture of the time. Holden lived thereafter as a farmer in the state of Washington. He died quietly in 1904.

MERIZO MASSACRE During World War II, as the American recapture of Guam approached, there were a number of atrocities committed by Japanese troops. The two most notorious are collectively known as the Merizo Massacre. On 15 July 1944, at Tinta near Merizo in southern Guam, sixteen Chamorros were murdered by the Japanese, and the following day at nearby Faha thirty more civilians were killed.

MICRONESIA: A GEOGRAPHICAL DEFINITION Micronesia encompasses an enormous area of the tropical, Western

Pacific Ocean. Land constitutes a mere 1,054 square miles within an oceanic region of well over 3 million square miles. Micronesia is one of the three major geographical regions or designations of the Pacific, or Oceania.

There are several island groups and individual islands in Micronesia: *mikros*, small; *nesos*, island, whose proposed name was submitted by Domeny de Rienzi to the *Societe de Geographic de Paris* in 1831. The island groups of Micronesia consist of the former Trust Territory of the Pacific Islands (TTPI) (q.v.), Guam (q.v.), Nauru (q.v.), and the Gilberts. The TTPI contains three major archipelagic areas: the Caroline Islands (q.v.), the Marshall Islands (q.v.), and the Mariana Island (q.v.). The vast east-west archipelago of the Caroline Islands includes five Micronesian states: Kosrae, Pohnpei, Chuuk, Yap, and Palau, respectively, of which the first four districts have formed a new political entity called the Federated States of Micronesia, numbering 957 islands, islets, and reefs, which total 461 square miles. The Marshall Islands, numbering 1,225 islands, islets and reefs, total 69.8 square miles. The Mariana Islands, exclusive of Guam, are now known as the Commonwealth of the Northern Marianas and number twenty-one islands, islets, and reefs, totaling 184.5 square miles.

Guam, the southernmost island of the Marianas archipelago, and its associated reef complexes, is approximately 214 square miles. Guam has been a U.S. territory (unincorporated) since 1898 and politically is separated from the other Marianas Islands and Micronesia.

The remaining Micronesian Islands are the Gilbert Islands, consisting of 114.12 square miles, and Nauru Island (an independent republic) which is 8.2 square miles.

Therefore, Guam and the islands of the former TTPI account for 929.8 square miles, which constitute approximately 88 percent of the total land area of Micronesia.

There are other physiographic characteristics of Micronesia that further distinguish the region from other areas of Oceania. Micronesia borders on East Asia and is part of a structural province known as the Western Margins. These "margins" refer to land divisions within the Pacific proper and the continental areas of Asia and Oceania.

In Micronesia the most significant physiographic distinction is established by the boundary between the Pacific Basin floor and the island structure (volcanic mountains) of the Philippine Sea. The Palau Islands, Yap Islands (excluding Ulithi and the other outer islands and atolls of Yap State), Guam and the Marianas, Kazan (formerly Volcano), Ogasawara (Bonin), and the Izu Islands to Honshu, Japan, constitute a section of the Andesite Line, which differentiates the deeper Pacific from the partially submerged continental areas on its margins.

The Western margins designate the complete area also known as the Pacific "Rim of Fire," where the Pacific Basin meets the trench adjacent to the island archipelagoes that convexly face the western Pacific along the Asian continent from Fiji to Palau to Japan. Therefore, Micronesian archipelagoes, that is, the Palaus, are located on the extreme eastern edge of Asia. Along this "edge," at or nearer the meridian 135 degrees east longitude, Koror and Tokyo are separated by 3,200 kilometers and provide a focus for a regional distinction. There is the Far East, including the countries of Indonesia, the Philippines, and Japan on the one hand, and the Western Pacific areas of Micronesia, including the outer islands of Yap, Chuuk, the Marshalls, and Nauru on the other.

MICRONESIAN AREA RESEARCH CENTER Created by an act of the Ninth Guam Legislature (q.v.) in 1967, the Micronesian Area Research Center (MARC) is situated at the University of Guam (q.v.) where it is a part of the Graduate School and an integral part of the academic community. MARC conducts social-science research of various kinds to acquire a better understanding of the area. It assists the various governments and agencies in the region in the preparation of special reports and surveys. It acquires historical and cultural relics for study and display. It publishes material of relevance to the area that will enhance cultural and historical understanding as well as understanding within the various social sciences and also publishes materials in support of instructional programs. MARC possesses a large 40,000-volume collection of archival materials, books, manuscripts, documents, microforms, photographs, periodicals, maps, and other materials related to Micronesia. The center also translates, transcribes, and prepares analytical bibliographic listings of important Spanish, German, French, Japanese, and other foreign-language documents. Members of the MARC faculty offer various graduate and undergraduate courses in the various colleges at the University of Guam.

MICRONESIA: A POLITICAL DEFINITION The small islands of Micronesia have a geographical, cultural, and political significance. Geographically, they encompass the Marianas, Carolines, Marshalls, Gilbert Islands, and Nauru.

Culturally, Micronesia includes generally the same groups, although there is a heavy Polynesian influence at Kapingamarangi Atoll, which is near the equator south of Truk (Chuuk) and Pohnpei, and a Melanesian influence at Tobi Island in Palau. Some ethnographers have considered Tuvalu (Ellice Islands) to be culturally Micronesian.

Politically, the definition is more complicated. Until recently Micronesia was usually considered synonymous with the United States-administered Trust Territory of the Pacific Islands (q.v.), which included all the Marshalls, Carolines, and Marianas except Guam (q.v.). Guam has been a U.S. possession since 1898 and an unincorporated territory of the United States since 1950.

In 1969 the people of the Trust Territory of the Pacific Islands entered into formal future political status negotiations with the United States. In 1972 the people of the Northern Mariana Islands broke away from the rest of the island groups and entered separate negotiations with the United States government, and subsequently, the Commonwealth of the Northern Mariana Islands (CNMI) was formed. The first governor, Carlos Camacho (q.v.), took office on 9 January 1978 at Saipan. Hence, the Mariana Islands now contain two political entities; Guam, a territory; and the Commonwealth, which is all the rest of the Mariana Islands.

The other island groups in the trust territory held a constitutional convention in 1975. The people voted on the adoption of this document on 12 July 1978. Four districts ratified: Yap, Pohnpei, Truk, and Kosrae. Two did not: Palau and the Marshall Islands. The four ratifying formed the Federated States of Micronesia (FSM) (q.v.), and their government, with an elected president, Tosiwo Nakayama, and a vice president, Petrus Tun, came into being officially on 10 May 1979. Elected as governor in each of the four states in the federation were Leo Falcam of Pohnpei, John Mangafel of Yap, Erhart Aten of Truk, and Jacob Nena of Kosrae.

The Marshall Islands drafted and had accepted by their people a constitution, which was passed in referendum in March 1979. In April an election was held for their new legislature, called the *Nitijela.* It has thirty-three members and provides for the election of one president, who is also a member of the legislative branch. There is no vice president. Amata Kabua was chosen as the first president and was inaugurated on 1 May 1979.

In April 1979 the Palauans also held a constitutional convention. Their document provides for a general election of president and vice president.

As it then existed, the Trust Territory of the Pacific Islands consisted of four separate government entities: the Northern Marianas (CNMI), the Marshall Islands, the Federated States of Micronesia (FSM), and Palau (Belau). Palau, however, had not yet ratified its Compact of Free Association with the United States, and so remained a trusteeship.

MICRONESIAN OCCUPATIONAL COLLEGE (MOC) Part of the Community College of Micronesia (q.v.) System, the Micronesian Occupational College is formerly the Micronesian Occupational Center, constructed in Palau in 1969–1970. The school is intended to train Micronesian students in vocational areas such as refrigeration repair, automobile repair, commercial cooking, and small engine repair. The enrollment was over 500 in 1992.

MODEKNGEI Modekngei is a religion in Palau, founded in the early 1900s by a man named Temedad from the village of A'ol. Modekngei means "to bring them together," referring to both the ancestral spirits and the Palauan people. Religious authority is derived from the ancient Palauan god, Ngiromokuul. Modekngei began as a political movement as well as a religious doctrine, and it was always anti-foreign. Temedad began his preachings at the end of the German administration and continued on into the Japanese period. He was thought to have occult powers through the performance of various feats and the experiencing of strange occurrences. In 1916 Temedad had what was probably an epileptic seizure and during which, he said, he communicated with Ngiromokuul, whom he claimed empowered him to dictate taboos. Subsequently, he declared that all traditional Palauan money was "contaminated" due to Japanese presence. Many brought their money to Temedad to be cleansed, for which he exacted a fee; some "unpurifiable" money he kept. He soon gained prestige and considerable wealth. A'ol became the center of Modekngei authority, and people came to pay tribute. Temedad recalled old political rivalries, settled arguments, cast out demons, and reportedly raised one woman from the dead. Soon the Japanese hospital became unpopular and patients were brought to Temedad instead. In 1918, on his orders, a school in Ngaraard was burned. Temedad proposed to unite all Palauans against foreigners, and all these activities were attempts to assert a conception of the old order of Palau, a society that the Japanese sought to change.

Today Modekngei still survives, although in more constructive forms, and many Palauans are adherents. (See Palau, Republic of)

MORI KOBEN (1869–1945) Japanese trader and colonialist who arrived at Truk (Chuuk) in 1892 aboard the *Tenyu maru.* He became involved in local native rivalries and became a military adviser to Manuppis, the most important chief on Moen Island in the Truk lagoon. He then settled on Moen and formed a private army. He married the daughter of Chief Manuppis, whose name was Isa, and she bore him twelve children. He learned to speak the Trukese language and to survive profitably in the culture.

When the German administration began in Micronesia in 1899, Mori was one of the Japanese businessmen and traders who was permitted to continue his trading efforts. When the

Japanese administration began in 1914, he eventually became an important adviser to the Japanese South Seas government. Mori died in Truk in 1945, leaving over sixty direct descendants.

MORNING STAR Four years after the Micronesian mission had been established, the sponsoring American Board of Commissioners for Foreign Missions (ABCFM) (q.v.) acquired a vessel in Boston, christened it *Morning Star,* and sent it to Hawaii in 1856 to become its link with Micronesia. The missionary packet carried mail, freight, and passengers on yearly cruises from its home port in Honolulu to all stations in Micronesia and, for a time, to those in the Marquesas as well. It was the first of seven ships to carry the name and to perform a similar service. The vessels were paid for, in part at least, by Sunday school children. Shares cost ten cents and entitled the shareholders to certificates.

The ships were not immune to problems faced by others in those Micronesian waters. *Morning Star I* simply wore out and was sold in 1866. A new one was built in East Boston, but in 1869 midway through its third cruise, *Morning Star II* drifted onto a reef at Kosrae where a squall finished it off. *Morning Star III* was launched at East Boston in 1871. It served thirteen years before wrecking in nearly the same spot as its predecessor. The distance covered during its 1881 cruise was logged at 15,783 miles. Another generation of Sunday school children provided enough dimes to build *Morning Star IV,* launched at Bath, Maine, in 1884. It was nearly twice as large as the last, and its passengers no doubt welcomed such innovations as a hurricane deck and auxiliary engines. The ABCFM hoped it would be the last, for expenses increased yearly. Nevertheless, *Morning Star V* had to be purchased in 1904. Home station was now in Micronesia, but it was more costly than ever to maintain this ship, and it was sold in 1906. Under German rule, commercial shipping in Micronesia improved and allowed the ABCFM to go out of the *Morning Star* business for good, it hoped. Following World War II, however, the ABCFM assumed temporary responsibility for churches in Micronesia until they could become self-sustaining. The Reverend Eleanor Wilson accepted delivery at Kosrae in 1948 of *Morning Star VI,* a used schooner purchased in Maine. In 1952 the vessel was condemned and sank at sea while being towed. *Morning Star VII* arrived in 1956, but like its predecessor, was not sound enough to perform well. In 1958, too battered to be dependable, this last of the *Morning Stars* was sold. (See Doane, Edward T.; Logan, Robert W.; Sturges, Albert)

N

NAKAYAMA, TOSIWO (1931–) Born on 23 November 1931, Piserach, Truk (Chuuk), Nakayama attended the University of Hawaii from 1955–1958 and from 1967–1969. He was an adviser to the United Nations delegation to Chuuk in 1961, and a member and president of the Truk District Legislature from 1963 to 1964. He was assistant district administrator for Public Affairs in Truk from 1964–1965, and later president of the Senate of the First Congress of Micronesia (q.v.) in 1965. In 1979 he was elected the first president of the Federated States of Micronesia (FSM) (q.v.).

NAN MADOL One of the most important archaeological attractions of Micronesia are the ruins of Nan Madol. A prehistoric city of man-made islands, Nan Madol is located at the mouth of the Madolenihmw Harbor on the island of Pohnpei in the eastern Carolines. The name Nan Madol translates as "the place between the spaces" and refers to the watery channels that flow among the more than 100 individual islets. Sometimes called the "Venice of the Pacific," the site is spread over an area of more than a quarter of a square mile. High-walled rectangular structures made from prismatic boulders of columnar basalt rock enclose the remains of old houses and administrative structures. On many of the islands tombs, tunnels, and underground chambers are found.

According to Pohnpeian tradition, two magicians from outside of Pohnpei built the site and established a dynasty of rulers known as the Saudeleurs. The Saudeleurs ruled Pohnpei from Nan Madol for several centuries until invaders from the island of Kosrae some 350 miles to the east conquered the city and established the existing system of Nanmwarkis, or "kings." Nan Madol remained the capital of Pohnpei until the eighteenth century. By then, disease, wars, and natural disasters forced the abandonment of the city. The Nanmwarki of Madolenihmw, the bloodline descendant of Isokelekel, commander of the Nan Madol invading forces, still holds authority over Nan Madol to this day.

Many outside visitors from countries all over the world down through the centuries have observed and described Nan Madol in literature, and there have been a number of scientific expeditions to the site. But Nan Madol's mysteries have never been completely unlocked. (See Lelu Ruins)

NANPEI, HENRY (1862–1928) The richest and most prominent Pohnpeian of the late nineteenth and early twentieth centuries was Henry Nanpei. He was the son of the Naniken, or "prime minister," of Kiti municipality. Nanpei attended school at the Protestant Mission at Oa and later in Hawaii. After returning to Pohnpei, Nanpei used his father's wealth and position to set up a trading business with the growing number of foreign commercial vessels plying Micronesia. The business prospered, and Nanpei soon opened a store in Kiti. With the goods received in return for supplying the ships, Nanpei was able to add to his already large holdings of land. Nanpei sold these goods to Pohnpeians who had nothing to offer in exchange except their land. Such transactions soon made Henry Nanpei the single largest landholder and provided him with power equal to that of the Nanmwarkis, or "kings."

The name Nanpei was actually the sixth title in the Nanmwarkis line of succession, but Henry was so powerful that he simply took the title and made it his last name.

Some accounts of the period name Nanpei, a Protestant, as an instigator behind the Protestant-Catholic wars that raged on Pohnpei between 1887 and 1899. Spanish authorities arrested Nanpei several times with intent to banish him from the island; he was so powerful, however, that he was the only one able to quell the disturbances.

A man of extraordinary wealth, Nanpei made numerous trips across the Pacific, and in 1905 he journeyed around the world. He is credited with introducing many foreign goods and influences into Pohnpei, and certainly he was no friend of the colonial administrations of Spain, Germany, and Japan. Henry Nanpei died in 1928, espousing an American protectorate for Pohnpei, something that would not come to his island for another 20 years.

NAN'YO BOEKI KAISHA (SOUTH SEAS TRADING COMPANY) During the Japanese administration of Micronesia, the Nan'yo Boeki Kaisha, or South Seas Trading Company, was the largest trading company in Micronesia. A private company, it was given a number of government contracts for the provision of transportation by means of a regional steamship line. The company was primarily involved in copra (q.v.) trading, but as it grew in the islands, it branched out into a number of other ventures until it became a large conglomerate. It is also known as NBK and was nicknamed "Nambo." Just prior to the onslaught of the Pacific war, the NBK was amalgamated with the government company, Nan'yo Kohatsu Kaisha, or South Seas Development Company (NKK), which was nicknamed "Nampo."

NAURU The Republic of Nauru is a small island (8.2 square miles) in the central Pacific, lying about twenty-five miles south of the equator. Its 1989 estimated population was 9,350.

Nauru was settled by Micronesian peoples from the Gilbert (q.v.), Caroline (q.v.), and Marshall (q.v.) islands. The first European to visit the island was John Fearne in 1798, who named it Pleasant Island because of the friendly welcome he received. Beginning around 1830, Nauru became a popular stop for food and water for whaling ships. Nauru was annexed by Germany in 1888 at the urging of German traders on the island. In 1914, shortly after the outbreak of the first World War, Nauru was captured by Australian forces. It continued to be administered by Australia under a League of Nations mandate (granted in 1920), which also named the United Kingdom and New Zealand as cotrustees. Between 1942 and 1945, Nauru was occupied by the Japanese. In 1947 the island was placed under United Nations trusteeship, with Australia as the administering power. Nauru received a considerable measure of self-government in 1966 with the establishment of legislative and executive councils, and became an independent country on 31 January 1968.

Nauru's economy is based on the mining, processing, and export of phosphate. Some of the revenue from phosphate sales has been invested in a long-term trust fund, in the development of shipping and aviation services, and in property purchases in Australia, Guam, Saipan, and elsewhere. Nauru's per capita income is among the highest in the world, due mostly to the phosphate earnings.

Nauru's president is elected by the eighteen-member parliament. Members of parliament are themselves elected every three years. The Nauru Local Council also provides governmental functions. The Council elects one of its members to be Head Chief. Adults twenty years of age or older must vote, voting being compulsory. (See Phosphate Mining)

NAURUAN ADMINISTRATORS

Brigadier General T. Griffiths	June 1921–June 1927
W. A. Newman	June 1927–January 1933
Commander Rupert C. Garsia	January 1933–October 1938
Lieutenant Colonel F. R. Chalmers	October 1938–March 1943
M. Ridgway	September 1945–August 1949
H. H. Reeve	August 1949–November 1949
R. S. Richards	November 1949–January 1953
J. K. Lawrence	January 1953–June 1954
R. S. Leydin	July 1954–May 1958
J. P. White	May 1958–April 1962
R. S. Leydin	May 1962–May 1966
Brigadier L. D. King	May 1966–January 1968

NAURUAN PRESIDENTS

Hammer DeRoburt	May 1968
Bernard Dowiyogo	December 1976
Lagumot Harris	April 1978
Hammer DeRoburt	May 1978
Kennan Adeang	September 1986

Hammer DeRoburt	October 1986
Kennan Adeang	December 1986
Hammer DeRoburt	January 1987
Kenas Aroi	August 1989
Bernard Dowiyogo	December 1989

NEW LIFE, OPERATION Operation New Life was the relocation program for Vietnamese refugees fleeing Vietnam following the 1975 Communist victory in the war. Guam was a staging area for the operation. The first plane of refugees arrived on 23 April, with the daily number of arrivals topping 5,000 during May. In all, over 100,000 Vietnamese transitted through Guam to new lives in the United States.

NGATIK MASSACRE, 1837 In July 1837 a band of European seamen and about twenty Pohnpeians, all armed with muskets, killed virtually the entire male population of Ngatik Atoll in the Caroline Islands. Many of the women killed their children and committed suicide after the slaughter. The leader of the whites, Charles "Bloody" Hart, captain of the *Lambton,* had attempted to trade at Ngatik the previous year. He and his trading party had been attacked and forced to flee. Hart returned in part from a desire for revenge on the islanders for this attack. The killing took place over a two-day period; about fifty to sixty Ngatikese men died.

NIMITZ, CHESTER W., ADMIRAL (1885–1966) American Naval officer Chester Nimitz was born in Fredericksburg, Texas. He graduated from Annapolis in 1905, and rose through the grades to rear admiral in 1938. He was chief of the bureau of navigation when, after the Japanese attack on Pearl Harbor, he was placed in command of the Pacific Fleet with the rank of admiral. He helped shape the American tactic of "island hopping." Under his command the fleets checked the Japanese advance at Coral sea and Midway; occupied or cut off the Japanese posts in Micronesia; and ultimately crushed Japanese sea power. Nimitz was made Admiral of the fleet in 1944 and signed on behalf the United States at the surrender ceremonies in Tokyo Bay aboard the battleship *USS Missouri* in 1945. He became chief of naval operations in 1945 and retired in 1947. He was named head of the Truman commission on internal security and individual rights in 1951.

NORTHERN MARIANAS, CAROLINES, AND MARSHALLS, COLONIAL GOVERNORS

German

Rudolph von Benningsen, 1899–1902
Albert Hahl, 1902–1914

Japanese

Tezuka Toshiro, 1921–1923
Yokoda Kosuke, 1923–1931
Horiguchi Mitsusada, 1931
Tawara Kazuo, 1931–1932
Matsuda Masayuki, 1932–1933
Hayashi Hisao, 1933–1936
Kitajima Kenjiro, 1936–1940
Kondo Shunsuke, 1940–1943
Hosokaya Ishiro, 1943–1944
(See Germany in Micronesia; Japan in Micronesia)

NUCLEAR TESTS Bikini and Eniwetak atolls in the Marshall Islands were used by the United States for tests with nuclear weapons, Bikini from 1946 to 1958 and Eniwetak from 1948 to 1958. Altogether there were sixty-six bomb blasts. The inhabitants of Eniwetak were evacuated before the tests began and were allowed to return to the atoll in 1980, after much of the contaminated area had supposedly been rendered safe. In 1992 the United States declared that Bikini was also safe for inhabitation.

O

O'CONNELL, JAMES F. (ca. 1808–1854) The celebrated "Tatooed Irishman," O'Connell arrived at Pohnpei in an open boat with several other sailors about 1830. He lived among the Pohnpeians until 1833. During his stay he was tattooed in the traditional Pohnpeian fashion. He later toured the United States as a curiosity, and in 1836 he published an account of his Pacific adventures. He performed in circuses and theaters until his death in New Orleans.

His account of Pohnpei was the first based upon an extended visit, but it must be read with some caution. Among the valuable descriptions of Pohnpeian culture there are exaggerations and incorrect remarks. Nonetheless, it is an important treatment of Pohnpeian culture before it was disturbed by European contact. (See Beachcombers; Tattoos and Tattooing)

O'KEEFE, DAVID DEAN (?–1903) Born in Ireland, O'Keefe emigrated to the United States as a young man. He was a blockade runner out of Savannah, Georgia, during the American Civil War. In 1871 he washed ashore at Yap following a shipwreck. He was nursed back to health, sailing away for Hong Kong early in 1872. Soon he was back on Yap where he developed a system of trade that exploited a traditional Yapese need: stone money from Palau. O'Keefe employed men to work the quarries on Palau, shipped the huge stones to Yap, and traded them for copra (q.v.) and bêche-de-mer (q.v.). He soon had a thriving business. His success led to jealousy from other white traders, and he was a favorite target for their recriminations. O'Keefe was the defendant in four of the five cases the British warship *HMS Espiegle* was sent to investigate in 1883. The charges against him were proved to be unfounded. Although other traders kept trying to compete with him, in the end it was "His Majesty" O'Keefe who won the battle for the lucrative Yap copra trade. He died at sea in 1903, leaving behind an estate worth over half a million dollars.

P

PACIFIC BASIN MEDICAL OFFICERS TRAINING PROGRAM (PBMOTP) The PBMOTP is a program of the U.S. Public Health Service, administered by the John A. Burns

School of Medicine of the University of Hawaii. Some 100 students were enrolled in 1988 to be trained as medical officers for all states in Micronesia. Medical officers are licensed to practice medicine within Micronesia but not outside of the region. The PBMOTP has practicum centers throughout the region and also a special cooperative arrangement with the Fiji School of Medicine.

PACIFIC ISLANDS TEACHERS TRAINING SCHOOL (PITTS) This is the successor to the Marianas Islands Teacher Training School (MITTS), which had been established on Guam in 1947 to train Micronesian teachers from all districts throughout the Trust Territory. Teacher training was moved to Truk from Guam in order to have the facility more centrally located within the Trust Territory. Teacher trainees from all over Micronesia came to PITTS for study. Eventually, the school was renamed the Pacific Islands Central School (PICS) as it became more of a general secondary education institution. In 1959 the school moved to Pohnpei.

PALAU, REPUBLIC OF The Republic of Palau is the westernmost cluster of the six major island groups that make up the Caroline Islands. Palau lies about 7 degrees and 30 minutes north of the equator and roughly 600 miles east of the Philippines. New Guinea lies to the south, and Guam is to the northeast. The Palau archipelago stretches over 400 miles in a north-south direction from the Atoll of Kayangel to the Islet of Tobi. At its greatest width, its major island reaches fifteen miles across.

The Palau Islands include more than 200 islands of which 8 are permanently inhabited. With three exceptions, all of the Palau Islands are located within a single barrier reef. This fact has made for a cultural homogeneity and relative ease of communication within the area.

Following World War II Palau became a part of the Trust Territory of the Pacific Islands (TTPI) (q.v.), which included the Marshall Islands, the rest of the Carolines, and the Marianas, which were formerly held by Japan (1914–1944). The U.S. Interior Department administered the Trust Territory and in 1956 granted Palau the opportunity to establish its own legislature, which is called the *Olbiil Era Kelulau* (Chamber of Whispered Decisions). In 1969 the Trust Territory peoples, including Palau, began negotiations toward a future political status with the United States. During the administration of President Gerald R. Ford in 1975, the status of Free Association was decided upon. A constitutional convention was held and the various island groups voted for ratification. Only Truk (Chuuk), Yap, Kosrae, and Pohnpei voted in favor of adoption and so these groups formed the Federated States of Micronesia (FSM) (q.v.) while Palau and the Marshalls remained separate and thus moved to ratify their own constitutions and to negotiate separate Compacts of Free Association with the United States.

The Palau constitution is patterned after that of the United States, although it is a uniquely Palauan document, both liberal and restrictive. It is liberal in granting Palauan citizens a high degree of personal freedom and protection and an enlightened government. It is restrictive in guarding the environment and Palauans rights to their scarce land and water resources.

The constitution sets up a democratic representative form of government organized into three branches: executive, legislative, and judicial. The executive branch is headed by a president, who is elected to a four-year term, as is the vice president. The president is assisted by his cabinet, consisting of the ministers of state, justice, administration, social services, and natural resources. The vice president serves as one of these ministers. The president is also advised on matters concerning traditional laws of Palau by a council of chiefs appointed in the traditional manner from each state.

The *Olbiil Era Kelulau* (OEK) is a bicameral congress with a house of delegates composed of one delegate from each of the sixteen states, and a senate, its eighteen members elected from senatorial districts based on population. Members of these bodies are elected for four-year terms. Sessions are convened regularly four times a year for twenty-five calendar days, and special sessions are called by either the president or the OEK leadership.

The judicial power of Palau is vested in a unified judiciary, consisting of a supreme court, a national court, and inferior courts. The supreme court is a court of record, having an appellate division and a trial division. Judges are appointed by the president from a list of nominees submitted to him by the judicial nominating commission, and all justices of the supreme court and judges of the national court hold their offices for life upon condition of good behavior.

The constitution provides for state governments following democratic principles and the traditions of Palau not inconsistent with the constitution. Unlike the United States constitution, which reserves powers not expressly delegated to the national government to the states and people, the Palau constitution reserves to the national government all the powers not expressly delegated to the states. This provides for a strong national government thought by the drafters of the constitution to be suitable to Palau's small size.

The Palau Compact of Free Association is a document negotiated by the government of the United States with the government of Palau. When it is ratified by the Palauan electorate, it will provide for the relationship between Palau and the U.S. for a designated period of time before a renegotiation will be necessary.

Palau is also known as Belau. This form is the traditional way of expressing Palau and is called for only when one is speaking Palauan. When speaking English or a language other than Palauan, Palau is the correct form.

PALAUAN PRESIDENTS

1982–1985	Hauro Remeliik
1985–1986	Alphonso Oiterong
1986–1988	Lazarus Salii
1988–1989	Thomas O. Remengesau
1989–	Ngiratkel Etpison

PALAUAN STORYBOARDS Storyboards have evolved from the traditional Palauan custom of carving stories on the beams, posts, and other parts of the interiors of *bais,* Palauan community houses. In the 1920s Hijikata Hisataku, a Japanese anthropologist, encouraged Palauans to carve and paint the stories on small pieces of wood so they could be used in trade. Hijikata called this new form ''itabory,'' later Americans used the term ''storyboard.''

PALOMO Y TORRES, JOSE BERNARDO (1836–1919) Padre Jose Palomo y Torres was born in Agana, Guam, on 19 October 1836, the only son of Don Sylvestre Palomo and Dona Rita Torres. His early life was spent studying under Father Pedro Leon del Carmen, pastor of Inarajan and Father Aniceto Ibanez in Agana. Padre Palomo studied for one year at San Carlos Seminary in Cebu in the Philippines before being ordained a priest on 11 December 1859. He was the first Chamorro to be ordained. He returned to Guam where his first assignment was as assistant to the curate of Agana. Over the next three decades he labored in Saipan, Tinian, and Rota. In 1895 he was again in Agana where he would remain until his death.

When the Americans occupied Guam after 1898, Padre Palomo did much to ease the apprehensions of the people of the island. He was held in high esteem by the American Naval administrators. Pope Pius X named him a papal chamberlain with the tile of Very Reverend Monsignor.

PEACE CORPS An international project of the United States government, the Peace Corps goals are: (1) to help the peoples of underdeveloped countries in meeting their needs for trained manpower; (2) to promote a better understanding of the American people on the part of the people served; and (3) to promote a better understanding of other peoples on the part of Americans.

Begun in 1961 under the direction of President John F. Kennedy, it was not until 1966 that some 350 Peace Corps volunteers arrived in Micronesia and the Pacific. In 1967 volunteers also began service in Tonga, Fiji, and Western Samoa. Later, groups were requested and sent to the Solomon Islands. Volunteers also served in the Cook Islands and in Vanuatu (the New Hebrides) under the auspices of the South Pacific Commission.

In all Pacific area countries, the initial program emphasized school education and public health. By 1968 there were some 800 volunteers and trainees in Micronesia alone, which represented the Peace Corps largest program strength per capita of anyplace in the world. In some Pacific countries, school enrollments rose dramatically with the arrival of primary-school English teachers. From 1966 to 1971 about 3,500 Peace Corps Volunteers from the United States served in the Pacific in some twenty different programs in nearly every major activity.

Most of the program concentrations in the Pacific have been in the human services areas. The Peace Corps has never been charged with economic development per se. All Pacific area volunteers receive training in local language, culture, and the technical area they will be working with. Altogether, they have served as teachers, health workers, nurses, public works engineers, tourism and small business advisers, lawyers, civil engineers, journalists, agricultural workers, fisheries development workers, community development aides, transportation assistants, land management and forestry officers, sanitation specialists, as well as in other areas.

The United States bears most of the cost for training and maintaining the volunteers in the field, although each host country in the Pacific also contributes some share for their support. Although some of the volunteers have been trained and certified as professionals in their areas of expertise, most are interested generalists who have recently graduated from college and who have received brief, intensive training in a specialized area. There are also a number of older volunteers, both men and women, serving in the Pacific. Methodologies employed to assess the impact of the Peace Corps on a country's population have been generally more descriptive than empirical. During the years of the Peace Corps service in the Pacific, every governing group has commended the efforts of the volunteers.

PEASE, BENJAMIN (?–1874) Pease was an American trader. Vermont-born Pease first appeared in Micronesia in 1866 representing a Honolulu firm. For the next four years he attempted to establish a commercial empire in the northern Gilberts, southern Marshalls, and eastern Carolines. His unscrupulous business practices led to charges against him being made by other traders and missionaries. In 1870 the *USS Jamestown* was dispatched to investigate. Further testimony against Pease was collected in the Marshalls and eastern Carolines, but the trader himself was not found; Pease was in Samoa helping his sometime companion "Bully" Hayes (q.v.) in escaping authorities. When Pease returned to Pohnpei and learned of the warship's visit, he fled to the Bonins where he lived in relative obscurity for the next three years. In October 1874 his bloody body was discovered at the bottom of a canoe.

PELELIU, BATTLE OF, 1944 The American 1st Marine Division assaulted Peleliu in the Palau Islands on 15 September 1944. The name assigned to the operation was "Stalemate."

A long, steep ridge honeycombed with caves and covered with dense jungle dominated the terrain, and the island is surrounded by a coral reef. The Japanese took advantage of these features, putting up a stubborn defense. The last resistance was not overcome until 7 November. The battle cost the Americans 1,794 dead. Of the 13,000 Japanese defenders, only 302 survived.

PHOSPHATE MINING Phosphate deposits in the form of guano were discovered on some islands of the Carolines in Micronesia during the German administration. A mining company was started on Angaur in 1913, and Chinese coolie labor was imported from the German Leasehold on the Shantung Peninsula. Many Micronesians also were used as labor in the mines. Phosphate was mined at Rota in the Marianas by the Japanese after they took over all German colonies in Micronesia after World War I. Large deposits of phosphate have been mined from Nauru (q.v.) in the years following World War II.

PIGAFETTA, ANTONIO (1486–1534) Pigafetta was an aide to Magellan. Pigafetta accompanied Magellan (q.v.) on his voyage around the world. This expedition represented the first European contact with Micronesia, stopping at Guam in 1521. Pigafetta's importance lies in his detailed narrative of the voyage. It has been translated and printed in many editions. He died in Malta in 1534.

POBRE DE ZAMORA, JUAN (?–1615) Born in Spain, Pobre was a lay brother of a Franciscan order. In 1601 he jumped ship at Rota and lived among the Chamorros for seven months. He left a detailed account of the islanders way of life.

PORTUGUESE The Portuguese reached the Pacific via the eastward route across the Indian Ocean to the East Indies and into the Pacific probably as far as the Caroline Islands. Don Jorge de Menezes, Captain General of the Moluccas, went out from Ternate in 1526 in a ship commanded by Dioga da Rocha (q.v.). The pilot of this voyage was Gomez de Sequeira, and they raised some islands, which the pilot was allowed to name for himself, the Sequeria Islands. These islands may have been Palau or Yap.

PREHISTORIC INTERISLAND CONTACT There may have been native canoes plying the waters between certain islands in the Carolines and the Philippines very early in Spanish times and before, because the Micronesians generally were very excellent seamen, although the size of their crafts made any regular voyages improbable. Ruy Lopez de Villalobos, brother-in-law of the Viceroy Mendoza of Mexico, crossed the Pacific from Natividad, New Spain, to Mindanao in the Philippines on a voyage lasting from 1 September 1542 to 2 February 1543. Villalobos reported that when he stepped ashore at Fais in Yap, the islanders spoke to him in Spanish. (See Canoes)

Q

QUIPUHA (?–1669) Quipuha was the paramount Chamorro chief in Agana when the Jesuit missionaries arrived on Guam in 1668. As a sign of friendship he allotted them land in Agana on which to build a church, the first church to be built on

Guam. Quipuha also became the first adult Chamorro to be baptized. When he died shortly after the church was completed, he was buried in the church.

QUIROGA, JOSE DE (?–1720) Spanish military governor of Guam from 1680–1681, 1688–1690, and 1694–1696. Captain Quiroga received a military education and gained experience in European warfare before arriving at Guam in 1679. He waged a ruthless campaign against the Chamorros on the island, burning villages, killing many inhabitants, and forcing many others to flee to other islands. He was relieved of his duties as governor but was on Guam to lead the military expedition of 1684. Quiroga's last campaign, in 1694–1695, resulted in the final conquest of the Marianas. (See Chamorro Wars)

QUIROS, PEDRO FERNANDEZ DE (1565–1615) In 1595, Pedro Fernandez de Quiros arrived at what very likely is Pohnpei in the Eastern Caroline Islands. The geographic position he reported as six degrees north latitude and his description coincided closely to that island.

R

REMELIIK, HARUO (1934–1985) First elected president of Palau, Remeliik was a strong supporter of Micronesian unity. After Palau separated itself from the rest of Micronesia, Remeliik became an active member of the Palau Constitutional Convention. He had served in the Trust Territory Government for many years as an assistant district administrator.

RIOS, JOSE L. G. (1898–1983) Rios was a Guam educator. He was born in Agana and educated in Guam schools and at Oklahoma State University of Agriculture and Applied Science, Stillwater, Oklahoma. Rios began his teaching career in 1915 and held various teaching and administrative posts until his retirement in 1966. He was once referred to as

Guam's "other Mr. Education" [this in reference to Simon A. Sanchez (q.v.)].

ROCHA, DIOGA DA In 1525 Dioga da Rocha, a Portuguese captain, was sent by the governor of the Moluccas to lay claim to any lands that might lie to the north. During a storm he was blown off course and came upon some islands in nine or ten degrees north latitude. He named them Ilhas de Gomez de Sequeira. These probably were the islands of Ulithi Atoll in the Carolines. Rocha and his men spent four months in the islands.

ROGERS, WOODES (1678–1729) On 11 March 1710 the British privateer Woodes Rogers arrived at Guam with his fleet of four ships after a 58-day voyage across the Pacific. He came to harass the Spanish, and in this intent he sent a letter from his ship *Duke* to Guam Governor Don Juan Antonio Pimental, saying that he wished to purchase all the provisions that could be spared and that, furthermore, if the Spanish failed to deal with him he would blast their villages with his ships' guns.

Governor Pimental directly made a present to Captain Rogers of "four bullocks, limes, oranges, and coconuts." In return Rogers invited Governor Pimental and four of his officers aboard his ship for dining and entertainment. Later, Rogers and his officers also visited the palace in Agana and were given a feast of "more than sixty dishes" of various delicacies.

After these initial niceties it appears that the two men were on even terms and could proceed respectfully in dealing with each other. Captain Rogers made great, and sometimes gruff, demands for provisions because of the large size of his fleet, and before the week was out he actually purchased "15 small and lean cattle, 2 cows and calves, 60 hogs, 100 fowls," as well as "Indian corn, rice, yams, and coconuts." Pimental quickly agreed, wanting no trouble with the privateers.

Rogers and his men were also very impressed with the speed and workmanship of the Chamorro flying *proas,* which they saw all around them in the Guam and Rota waters. Captain

Rogers observed: "By what I saw, I believe they may run 20 miles an hour, for they passed our ships like a bird flying." When Rogers left Guam on 22 March 1710, he took one of the flying *proas* back to London with him as a souvenir. (See Canoes)

S

SAAVEDRA CERON, ALVARO DE (?–1529) Saavedra was a Spanish explorer who was the first European to cross the Pacific north of the equator. Hernan Cortez, a kinsman of Saavedra, ordered him to mount an expedition to the Moluccas to ascertain the fate of the Loaysa expedition. He sailed from Mexico in December 1527. On his voyage across the Pacific, he discovered Utirik, Taka, Rongelap, and Ailinginae in the Marshalls. He proceeded on to the Moluccas, picking up a few survivors of the Loaysa expedition in the Philippines. Saavedra then made two unsuccessful attempts to return to Mexico during which he discovered the islands of Pohnpei and Ant in the eastern Carolines and Ujelang and Eniwetak in the Marshalls. Saavedra died at sea before reaching Mexico.

SAFFORD, WILLIAM EDWIN (1859–1926) Safford was an American "vice governor" of Guam and a botanist. Born in 1859 and raised in Ohio, Safford attended the Naval Academy and was in the Navy during the Spanish-American War. Upon his arrival on Guam in 1899 as the aide to Governor Richard P. Leary (q.v.), he was instructed to do whatever he thought was necessary to administer the island and to call on the governor only in emergencies. Safford served as judge of the court of first instance, as judge of the criminal court, and as registrar of lands, deeds, and titles. After retiring from the Navy, he went on to a productive career as a botanist. His work *The Useful Plants of Guam* (1905) is a classic, being a virtual handbook of the island.

SAIPAN, BATTLE OF, 1944 American forces seized the Mariana Islands of Saipan, Tinian, and Guam because the Navy needed advanced bases for operations against the Philip-pines, and the Air Force needed fields from which B-29s could bomb Japan.

Saipan was the objective of the 2nd and 4th Marine Divisions and the 27th Army Infantry Division as reserve. D day was 15 June 1944. The landing on the beaches was met by heavy Japanese fire, which caused 2,000 casualties on the first day and required the commitment of the 27th Division.

By D plus 1, the 4th Division had attacked straight ahead and the 2nd Division had penetrated to Chalon Kanoa, the sugar mill town inland. On the morning of the 17th the Japanese mounted a heavy tank-led attack that caused con-siderable damage before it was stopped. By the 18th, the 4th Division had crossed the island to the east coast, while Army units began clearing out the southern end of the island.

On 20 June, as the 2nd Division wheeled in line to face the north, the 4th Division moved to the right side of the line and the 27th moved to the center in a coordinated drive to the northern tip of the island. When the attack of the Army Division bogged down, Lt. General Holland Smith, the Marine commander of the entire operation, removed the division's commander, Major General Ralph C. Smith, an act that generated considerable interservice controversy. The Army subsequently sustained Ralph Smith.

In the north part of Saipan the 4th and 27th Divisions pressed the attack. The north tip of the island was reached on 9 July when Saipan was declared secure. Here one of the most tragic events of the war occurred as entire families of civilians, egged on by Japanese soldiers, leaped to their deaths from the 220-foot cliff at Marpi Point.

SAKAU One of the traditionally favored drinks in the islands is kava. In Micronesia it is a popular drink on Pohnpei and is called *sakau* there. In Hawaii it is called kava, and *yangona* in Fiji. It is a nonalcoholic, euphoria-producing beverage made on most Pacific islands from the root of a plant in the pepper family that has the scientific name of *Piper methys-ticum*.

The effects of eating or drinking a preparation of this yellowish root have been variously described, with agreement that there are feelings of stimulation followed by sedation; sleepy intoxication of a melancholy, silent, and drowsy sort. Strong doses of *sakau* can cause loss of muscular control and also affect vision.

The root of *Piper methysticum* may be used dried or freshly dug. In Polynesia and in southern and eastern Melanesia, the root is either chewed or it is pounded and pulverized with a wooden beater. It is then infused in water and may be mixed by hand in a carved bowl or strained through a coconut spathe into a bowl or half-coconut shell. In Pohnpei, hibiscus bark fibers are wrapped around the beaten, moist pulp, and then twisted and wrung. The first cup of the resulting ooze is then given to the ranking members of the groups.

Kava/*sakau* use has many different cultural meanings throughout the Pacific relating to political structure and social status. In some cultures both men and women are allowed to prepare and drink the drug, in others only men are permitted to indulge.

In the past some governments in the islands have attempted to suppress kava /*sakau*. But most islanders advocate it as a traditional and acceptable alternative to alcohol and the problems of alcoholism in the Pacific. (See Alcohol in the Pacific; Betel Nut Chewing)

SALII, LAZARUS (1935–1988) The second elected president of Palau, Salii committed suicide on 20 August 1988. An early supporter of Micronesian political unity, Salii was obliged to support Palau separatism after the Federated States of Micronesia was established in 1978 and Palauans voted not to join. A strong advocate of the Compact of Free Association with the United States, Salii worked assiduously, but unsuccessfully, toward its passage by plebiscite. He became involved in various controversies surrounding the establishment of a large power plant in Palau built by a British Company called IPSECO, Inc.

SAN GERONIMO The *San Geronimo* was one of the early Manila galleons (q.v.) and was taken over by mutineers in 1567 while on a voyage to the Philippines. The captain and his company of loyalists overpowered the mutineers and then set them to their fate on some island. Accordingly, twenty-six were marooned somewhere in the Carolines on an island that came to be known as *Barbudos,* or island of the Bearded Ones. These men were never seen again, but many years later captains of the galleons were to hear stories from the natives about the men living in the Carolines. (See *San Pablo*)

SAN JUAN DE LETRAN The first school in Micronesia was built on Guam, and it was called El Colegio de San Juan de Letran. Located in Agana, San Juan de Letran was constructed of stone and mortar with a special fund of 3,000 pesos granted by Queen Mariana (q.v.) of Spain in 1669.

The school grew and prospered and trained the Chamorros and mestizos in reading, writing, and arithmetic. By 1727 the school had regular boarders, and fully half of the student body came from villages other than Agana, as well as from Rota and Saipan. The students were all boys and ranged in age from eight to twenty-seven years old.

All materials, books, paper, and ink pens were provided free for all, and meals and clothing were given to the boarders. The uniforms consisted of blue pullover vests and white pants with a white linen kerchief worn around the neck and a white sash around the waist.

Everyone at the school worked in some way or another. There was a copious garden with many varieties of vegetables and root crops grown. Pigs and chickens were raised. There was never a shortage of food and little was wasted. The boys got up at five to say their prayers, wash, and dress. After mass, chores, and breakfast of rice porridge, academic subjects were studied for two hours. Then the formal start of school was signaled by the ringing of a bell.

The catechism was taught and also useful crafts such as bookbinding, tailoring, embroidery, and masonry. Musical instruction was given for singing and some playing of the harp. There were games such as bowling, handball, and checkers. San Juan de Letran's students enjoyed an opportunity unparalleled in most parts of the world 250 years ago to obtain a formal education. (See Chamorro Education [Jesuit]; Spanish Mission Schools)

SAN PABLO The *San Pablo,* under the command of Miguel Lopez de Legazpi (q.v.), sailed from Acapulco, Spain, in 1564 to make formal claim for Spain of Guam and the Philippines. Aboard was the famous navigator Fray Andres Urdaneta (q.v.) who navigated the *San Pablo* back across the Pacific from the Philippines in 1565 to the North American coast and then southward to Acapulco. Thus, the *San Pablo* was the first of the Manila galleons (q.v.) to make the Pacific round-trip. (See *San Geronimo)*

SAN VITORES, DIEGO LUIS DE (1627–1672) Known among Roman Catholics today as ''The Apostle of the Marianas,'' San Vitores was born in Burgos, Spain, on 12 November 1627. He was admitted into the Society of Jesus in 1640 and entered the priesthood ten years later. San Vitores was assigned to several teaching posts in Spain until he left for missionary work in the Philippines in 1660. On 24 June 1665, the King of Spain, Don Felipe IV, signed a royal cedula authorizing evangelization of the Marianas. San Vitores, who had stopped at Guam in 1662, was selected to head the mission, arriving at Guam on 16 June 1668. The missionaries were at first welcomed with the Chamorro leader of Agana, Quipuha (q.v.), giving them land on which the Jesuits built a church. Problems soon arose, however, owing to differences in Chamorro and Spanish customs. Open conflict between the two groups broke out in 1671. On 2 April, San Vitores was murdered at Tumon by Matapang (q.v.) and an accomplice after the priest had baptized Matapang's daughter against the father's wishes. On 6 October 1985, Pope John Paul II beatified Father San Vitores.

SANCHEZ, SIMON A. (1895–1975) Born in Agana, Sanchez attended Guam public schools and took additional courses from the University of Chicago and the University of Hawaii. He served as a teacher, administrator, and board member in Guam's school for more than thirty years; he retired in 1959. He also was elected to the prewar Guam Congress (q.v.). He was known as Guam's ''Mr. Education.''

SANTA MARIA DE GUADALUPE On 6 June 1683, Guam Governor Antonio Saravia, in a letter to King Carlos II of

Spain said: "Since in the Marianas the typhoons destroy all wooden houses and buildings, I have decided to construct a fort out of stone, mortar and limestone." When the fort was completed Governor Saravia reported that it had a capacity for 400 men and contained armament of three cannons and a mortar. The fort was named Santa Maria de Guadalupe, and it was Guam's first permanent fort.

There was, however, a protective wood palisade built around the Spanish settlement in Agana about a dozen years before Governor Saravia's fort was finished. It was built by Captain Juan de Santa Cruz, Guam's first military governor of the Marianas. The exact location of the palisade is not known, but it was someplace in Agana. It was made of coconut logs and had a church and a house inside its walls. Two towers were built into the sides, one facing the sea and the other facing the nearby mountain. Each tower possessed armaments, and reportedly the whole palisade had 31 men as defenders.

The Spanish colonists needed the defenses as reflected by these fort constructions. The Chamorros had difficulty in accepting the strict codes of living demanded by Christianity and frequently rebelled violently when these Spanish codes came into conflict with the Chamorro culture.

Fort Guadalupe was the first of many Spanish forts on Guam, some of them impressive naval defenses, but Guadalupe's purpose was to defend the Spanish against the Chamorros, who, during the first 40 years of Spain's reign, were the greatest challenge. (See Chamorro Wars)

SECURITY CLEARANCE A required security clearance was imposed by U.S. military authorities for entrance into Guam or the Trust Territory of the Pacific Islands (q.v.) prior to 1962. During the 1950s, the Trust Territory maintained secure facilities at Kwajalein for missile testing, and at Saipan for Naval Technical Training Units (NTTU); therefore, all persons wanting to enter the region needed a clearance.

In the case of Guam, the presence of six major military base facilities with nuclear weapons present further required security clearances for entry. Even native Chamorros needed such a clearance to return to their island homes from overseas. The security clearance requirement was lifted in 1962 during the administration of President John F. Kennedy.

SEMPER, CARL GOTTFRIED (1832–1893) Carl Semper wrote one of the finest firsthand accounts of Palauan culture entitled *Palau Islands in the Pacific Ocean,* which was published in Leipzig in 1873. Unlike many other nineteenth-century explorers in Micronesia, Semper remained long enough, from March 1862 through January 1863, to gain his knowledge through observation rather than only from informants. Fortunately, Semper had the leisure, concern, and objectivity to write a fascinating description of traditional Palauan nature and culture before much of it vanished.

His *Palau Islands in the Pacific Ocean* contains the only known descriptions of some of the customs, feasts, and ceremonies of these Pacific islanders. His precise imagery reveals the craftsmanship used in distilling vast information scattered throughout his many notebooks and diaries into a well-written, novelistic autobiography that offers much to those interested in German Romantic literature on the one hand, and a serious discussion of culture change and a humane appreciation of Palauan life on the other.

SHENANDOAH In April 1865 the *Shenandoah,* a Confederate raider commanded by Lieutenant Commander James I. Waddel, arrived at Pohnpei. After putting the crews on shore, Waddel burned the four whale ships that were in port. He then sailed north to destroy more of the American whaling fleet. On leaving Pohnpei, Waddel recruited thirteen islanders to serve on his ship, undoubtedly the only Micronesians in the Confederate Navy.

SKINNER, CARLTON S. (1913–) Skinner was the first civilian governor of Guam, serving from 1949–1953. Born in California, Skinner was educated at Wesleyan University in Connecticut and the University of California, Los Angeles. He worked as a correspondent until World War II, during which he served in the U.S. Coast Guard. Skinner acted as special assistant to the secretary of the interior from 1947–1949. He successfully organized a civilian government for Guam after more than fifty years of United States Navy rule. His administration was noted for his cooperation with the Guam Legislature (q.v.) and for his appointment of Chamorros to high-level posts. A plaza in Guam's capital, Agana, is named in his honor. (See Guam, Organic Act of)

SOKEHS REBELLION In 1910, an event took place on the eastern Caroline island of Pohnpei that shocked the world. It was a violent, armed revolt by the Pohnpeians against their German masters known as the Sokehs Rebellion after the municipality in which it occurred. It was the last major uprising against foreign rule in Micronesia.

There had been a revolt in Pohnpei in 1890 against the Spanish. The German administration, which began in 1899 and lasted until 1914, was also resented by the Pohnpeians. Opposition to German land policies, dislike of the labor tax, and the use of corporal punishment all contributed to the uprising.

It was on the morning of 18 October 1910 that the trouble began. The Germans had been building a road and had beaten a Pohnpeian worker for alleged laziness. Seeing bruises on his body, the man's clansmen and relative came forth and threatened the German supervisor. When the German governor, Hans Boeder, tried to settle the dispute, he was shot in the stomach and the head and died instantly. The governor's male secretary, two road supervisors, and five Mortlock islanders were also killed.

The Germans retreated to the walled colony at Kolonia and called for reinforcements, which arrived after two months. Then, after another two months of pursuit, all the rebels were rounded up and a trial was held. Seventeen were sentenced to death and executed by firing squad on 24 February 1911. Rebel sympathizers and their families were exiled to Palau. The Germans took possession of their land and distributed it to island settlers from the Mortlocks and elsewhere in the Carolines. It was not until some ten years later during the Japanese administration that relatives and descendants of the rebels were allowed to return to Sokehs.

They were never permitted to reclaim their land, however. (See Soumadau)

SOLOMON REPORT Officially entitled "A Report by the U.S. Government Survey Mission to the Trust Territory of the Pacific Islands," the Solomon Report was issued in October 1963. President John F. Kennedy had appointed Professor Anthony N. Solomon of Harvard University to head a government survey mission to the Trust Territory (q.v.) to review the major political, economic, and social problems facing the islanders. The mission was to gather information and make recommendations needed in the formulation of United States policies and programs to accelerate development in the region. The report itself was critical of past U.S. policies and proposed that Micronesians should be influenced to wish for a future political status as an American territory. This classified report was leaked to the press and created a climate of distrust among Micronesians.

SOUMADAU (?–1911) He was the leader and tactician in the Sokehs Rebellion (q.v.) against the German colonial administration at Pohnpei in the eastern Caroline islands in 1910. Soumadau was a high-ranking nobleman who was hired by Governor Hans Boeder to help supervise the free Pohnpeian labor drafted to build roads. Tension existed between the administration and the Sokehs people, and traditional "signs" had indicated that the Sokehs district would soon suffer annihilation.

On 17 October 1910, a German supervisor severely beat a laborer, and Soumadau and others agreed to avenge the dishonor. When approached the following day by the governor and aides, the Pohnpeians killed him, raided the colony for guns, and retreated to the mountaintop fortification, which all visitors can see today as Sokehs Rock.

Both sides apparently refused to negotiate, and beginning on 13 January 1911 combined naval bombardments and pincer attacks by German and Melanesian troops eventually drove the rebels into the interior. Dispersed and receiving little aid, groups of rebels gradually surrendered. Soumadau surrendered on 13 February to a neighboring Pohnpeian chief and was executed in Kolonia on 24 February 1911 along with fourteen other rebels who were collectively held responsible for Governor Boeder's death and the deaths of the others who had been with him on that fateful day of the previous October. Two other rebels were reportedly executed shortly thereafter on Yap.

With Soumadau's death, all armed resistance against the colonials ceased for good.

SPAIN Starting in 1519 with Magellan's (q.v.) circumnavigation, Spain explored the possibility of reaching the Spice Islands (Moluccas) by crossing the Pacific Ocean. After the discovery of the return route to the Americas in 1565, Spain established her domination over the Philippines, and later over Micronesia.

There were three main Spanish voyages to the Spice Islands: two from Spain and one from Mexico. Magellan emerged into the Pacific in 1520 after going through the straits that now bear his name. Crossing the Pacific was a great ordeal; no refreshments could be obtained before reaching Guam. Magellan was killed in the Philippines, but one of his ships, the *Victoria,* under the command of Juan Sebastian Del Cano (also El Cano), reached Spain in 1522, having sailed around the world.

The next expedition under Loaysa entered the Pacific in 1526, attempting to establish Spanish rule in the Spice Islands in spite of Portuguese objections. Loaysa and El Cano, who had gone with him, died while crossing the ocean. According to a theory espoused by Robert Langdon of Canberra, Australia, castaways from one of the ships intermarried with Polynesian women and even today Spanish features may be detected in their descendants.

Following a request from Emperor Carlos V, who ruled Spain, Cortes sent Alvaro de Saavedra Ceron (q.v.) from Mexico in 1527 to rescue Spaniards who had remained in the area of the Spice Islands. Saavedra found some of them fighting the Portuguese. He died unable to return to Mexico. Conflict over the Spice Islands was settled by the treaty of Saragossa in 1529 when Carlos V renounced his claims in exchange for money.

A number of Spanish vessels had made the crossing from east to west, but attempts to recross it had failed. The last one had been made by the *San Juan* of Villalobos's fleet in 1545. Unless a return route could be found, Spain could not hope to keep settlements in the western Pacific. A northern route of return was finally found in 1565, mainly through the skill of Fray Andres Urdaneta (q.v.) a survivor of Loaysa's expedition. Spain started colonization of the Philippines under Miguel Lopex de Legazpi's (q.v.) leadership. The islands were actually in Portugal's sphere, but Spain ignored Portuguese protests. For several decades, Spain and Portugal were ruled by the same monarch and some Spaniards wanted to conquer parts of the Asian mainland. Possession of the Philippines gave Spain a share in the wealth of Asia through the Manila galleon (q.v.) trade. Missionary work led Spain reluctantly to extend her rule over Micronesia in the second half of the seventeenth century. Up to that time only Guam had served as a port of call for ships. Spain's sway over Micronesia was never as firm as over the Philippines, and she had to reckon more and more with attacks from her European rivals.

Spain participated in the final stages of exploration in the Pacific. Her finest navigator of the time was Malaspina, who sailed all through the Pacific from 1790–1793. The scientists who accompanied him collected data that filled many volumes. After the loss of her American colonies, Spain discontinued the Manila galleon trade between Mexico and the Philippines, but kept in communication with these islands through other sea lanes. Toward the middle of the nineteenth century, there was restlessness in Spain and the Philippines and some liberals were deported to Micronesia. Spain had a series revolt on her hands in the Philippines when the Spanish-American War broke out. She lost the archipelago and Guam to the United States in 1898. The following year, she sold the islands of Micronesia she had claimed to Germany. After 1899 Spain's flag was not flying any longer on land owned by her in and around the Pacific Ocean.

SPANISH MISSION SCHOOLS Spanish mission schools were established throughout the Marianas beginning with El Colegio de San Juan de Letran (q.v.) in 1669. Other schools were established as early as 1674, and by the end of the Spanish period, every village had a school. The majority of the Spanish priests sent to the Marianas were Basques who taught a rigid medieval Christianity.

Along with the indoctrination of the Catholic faith, the curriculum included reading, writing, arithmetic, Spanish, music, and handicrafts. (See Chamorro Education [Jesuit])

STICK CHARTS These were navigational aids used to travel from one island to another out of sight of land. They were fashioned of bamboo with shells used to represent islands. The charts indicate wave patterns, winds, and current. Many stick charts are now found in the world's museums.

STURGES, ALBERT (1817–1887) Albert Sturges was the first American Protestant missionary to come to Micronesia. He was a graduate of Wabash College, Crawfordsville, Indiana, and Yale Seminary and came to Pohnpei in 1852 along with his wife, Susan, aboard the schooner *Morningstar* (q.v.), the first sailing ship of the mission. The Sturgeses established the first mission for the Congregationalists at Kiti municipality. For some eighteen years Reverend Sturges led the other missionaries and Pohnpeian converts in the work of Bible translation, the training of local pastors, and the building of churches throughout the region.

After a home visit, the Sturgeses returned to Pohnpei in 1871 and extended their mission work to the islands of Mokil and Pingelap. In 1874 they established another mission in the Mortlocks. At last, in 1879 a mission was established at Truk, a place that had previously been a difficult place for missionaries to enter. Dr. Sturges was helped in this effort by a Pohnpeian named Moses whom he and his wife had adopted as a child. Moses remained in Truk to assist with the settlement and was quite successful.

The Sturgeses remained on Pohnpei throughout the 1870s, making yearly visits to mission stations in Truk, the Mortlocks, and throughout Pohnpei district. After a furlough to the United States in 1882, Sturges returned to the mission at Pohnpei and continued his work until a stroke forced his and his wife's retirement in 1885. Albert Sturges died in 1887, having played an instrumental part of the Protestant missionization of the Eastern Carolines. (See American

Board of Commissioners for Foreign Mission; Doane, Edward T.; Logan, Robert W.)

T

TAITANO, FRANCISCO SAN NICOLAS (1892–1937) Born on Guam, Taitano organized the first school for teaching English during the early years of the American administration. Governor Dorn, in 1909, awarded him a medal for his efforts. He was appointed Secretary to the Guam Congress (q.v.) in 1925, and was himself elected to that body in 1931. He also compiled an English-Chamorro dictionary. In 1919 Taitano established the first private school on Guam.

TATTOOS AND TATTOOING Tattoos originated in the Pacific Islands and were often used in place of clothing. Tattoos were not arbitrary but had clear cultural and social meaning. Tattooing was accomplished by dipping fish bones and sharp shells into plant dyes. Tiny hammers or mallets were also used to drive the color into the skin. It often took days and even weeks to complete large body tattoos.

Intricate cultural designs for tattoos were collected by early European naturalists and other visitors to the islands. Islanders would sometimes forcibly tattoo outsiders such as the captured American whalers Benjamin Knute and William Hussey in 1832 on Tobi Island, Palau. The traditional practice of tattooing has all but vanished in Micronesia, although occasional efforts at revival are seen. (See *Mentor; O'Connell, James F.*)

TETENS, ALFRED (1839–18?) A German trader who arrived at Truk in 1868 aboard his ship *Vesta,* Tetens, like the British trader Andrew Cheyne (q.v.) who preceded him, reported that his ship was almost taken in a surprise attack by Trukese who had come aboard ostensibly to trade with the crew. Tetens reported that he himself grappled with the Trukese instigator and threw him overboard by the legs.

Tetens also traded in Palau and other Caroline islands before returning to Germany where he eventually served as port captain in Hamburg, Germany.

TINIAN, BATTLE OF, 1944 American forces seized the Mariana Islands of Saipan, Tinian, and Guam because the Navy needed advance bases for operations against the Philippines and the Air Force needed fields from which B-29s could bomb Japan.

Saipan, which is only three miles north of Tinian, was already in American hands and thus could be used as a staging area for the assault on Tinian.

Tinian held three airfields with one more under construction. Scheduled to be invaded on 24 July 1944, Tinian received a heavy preinvasion bombardment.

The landing on Tinian was unique in that it was possible to take Marine unit commanders on reconnaissance flights over the objective. Another unusual aspect of this operation was that it was one of the few shore-to-shore landings of the war. Also, it was at Tinian that napalm was first used in the war. The landing went off as scheduled with the 4th Marine Division landing on the 24th. The 2nd Marine Division joined in the attack on the 26th. On 1 August, organized resistance ceased. In this operation, 317 Marines were killed as opposed to nearly 5,000 Japanese.

TOBIAS, MARIANO Tobias was governor of Guam from 1771–1774. An enlightened and humane ruler, Tobias was genuinely interested in the welfare of the Chamorros and aided them in many ways. He reformed agriculture in Guam by introducing new crops and allotting idle land to more families. Under his supervision the growing of rice, maize, cotton, indigo, cacao, sugarcane, and other crops was expanded. Cattle, horses, and donkeys were imported from America, and deer were introduced from the Philippines. He built cotton mills and salt pans, and brought in blacksmiths, carpenters, and other craftsmen to teach local men their skills. He established two public schools and the first Guam Militia. Visitors wrote highly of him, leading to a favorable reputation at court in Spain. This led to jealousy, and, combined with quarrels he had with missionaries, led to his removal.

TOURISM Guam is the tourist center of Micronesia with 784,018 visitors estimated in 1993. About 85 percent of Guam's tourists are Japanese. Most of the hotels are located on or near Tumon Bay where many of Guam's entertainment establishments are located.

The northern Marianas, especially Saipan, are the next most popular destination for tourists with about 300,000 visitors each year. Roughly 80 percent are from Japan.

Outside of the Marianas, tourism is of less importance to local economies. In Palau the industry is being developed, aimed at the Japanese market as on Guam and Saipan. Chuuk (Truk) is a favorite with scuba divers. In the Gilberts and Marshalls, attempts to develop tourism have been largely unsuccessful.

TREATY OF PARIS, 1898 The treaty between the United States of America and the Empire of Spain following the Spanish-American War, the Treaty of Paris was signed on 10 December 1898. Spain ceded the Philippines, Puerto Rico, and Guam (q.v.) to the United States for $20 million. (See United States Takes Control of Guam)

TREPANG See *Bêche-de-Mer*

TRUK (CHUUK), REDUCTION OF, 1944 Truk Lagoon, a thirty-eight-mile-wide lagoon in the Caroline islands, served as the headquarters and base of the Japanese Combined Fleet. Truk's importance lay in its strategic location combined with the naval and air strength it held. American planners decided to bypass Truk. Beginning on 17 February 1944, continual naval and air bombardment nullified the value of the base to the Japanese. In the first two days of attacks alone, over 130,000 tons of shipping were sunk. In all, twenty-three ships and 201 planes were destroyed at a cost of seventeen American aircraft. The Japanese withdrew their remaining aircraft to the Bismarck Islands.

TRUST TERRITORY OF THE PACIFIC ISLANDS (TTPI) The original Trust Territory of the Pacific Islands, established in 1947, covered some 3 million square miles of the western Pacific Ocean just above the equator, ranging from about 1 degree to about 22 degrees north latitude, and

130 degrees to 172 degrees east longitude. The TTPI embraced more than 2,000 islands and islets, lying in 3 major archipelagos: the Carolines (q.v.), the Marshalls (q.v.), and the Marianas (q.v.).

The TTPI was the only one of eleven trusteeships established by the United Nations after World War II that was designated as a "strategic" trusteeship. This rendered ultimate United Nations authority to reside with the Security Council rather than with the Trusteeship Council, although the latter handled the normal administration processes and annual reporting from the administering power.

Between 1978 and 1986, the TTPI was composed of four constitutional governments: the Republic of the Marshall Islands (q.v.), the Republic of Palau (q.v.), the Federated States of Micronesia (FMS) (q.v.), comprised of Truk (Chuuk), Pohnpei, Yap, and Kosrae, and the Commonwealth of the Northern Marianas (CNMI) (q.v.). With the abolition of the Office of High Commissioner in 1987, a residual Office of Transition was located on Saipan for the purpose of completing ongoing transfers of property and programs and generally closing down what was left of the Trust Territory Headquarters. This office was permanently closed on 30 September 1991, and the remaining TTPI functions were transferred to the director, Palau Office, TTPI.

TRUST TERRITORY OF THE PACIFIC ISLANDS, HIGH
COMMISSIONERS

Admiral Louis E. Denfield	1947–1948
Admiral Dewitt C. Ramsey	1948–1949
Admiral Arthur W. Radford	1949–1951
Elbert D. Thomas	1951–1953
Frank E. Midkiff	1953–1954
Delmas H. Nucker	1954–1961
M. W. Goding	1961–1966
William R. Norwood	1966–1969
Edward E. Johnston	1969–1976
Peter T. Coleman (acting)	1976
Adrian P. Winkel	1977–1980
Daniel High (acting)	1981
Janet J. McCoy	1981–1987

TWEED, GEORGE RAY (1902–1989) Tweed was a radioman who enlisted in the United States Navy in 1922 and who happened to be on Guam in December 1941 when the Japanese invaded the island. He fled into the jungle and eluded capture until July 1944 when an American warship rescued him. He owed his survival primarily to the Chamorros, who sheltered and aided him. Many persons were tortured or killed as the Japanese tried to find Tweed. A book, *Robinson Crusoe, USN,* was written about his exploits, which was later made into a motion picture, *No Man is an Island.*

U

UDOUD The traditional native monetary system for Palau is unique in Micronesia. Except for Yap, where traditionally large, aragonite stone disks are used for money, Palau's is the most highly developed and complex monetary system. The money itself consists of polychrome and clear glass beads, and crescentic bar gorgets, and beads of pottery. All these are generically called *udoud.* The ceramic and glass prismatic pieces are called *ba'al,* and the beadlike pieces are called *bleab.* Ceramic *udoud* is found in yellow, red, or orange varieties; the glass pieces come in a wide variety of colors and degrees of transparency. All *udoud* feature a hole through which a string or cord can be passed. All are of foreign importation.

Today, *udoud* have a strong influence on Palauan society and culture. This, despite the fact that no new *udoud* have been created or introduced in recent years and that the pieces are not used to make actual purchases. *Udoud* are most often given as gifts at ceremonies for weddings, births, funerals, and newly built houses. (See Kubary, Johann Stanislaus; Yapese Stone Money)

UNITED STATES COMMERCIAL COMPANY (USCC) A government company formed for the express purpose of providing food, clothing, shelter, and supplies for areas captured from enemies in World War II. In Micronesia, the

USCC set up branches in each district captured from the Japanese in 1944. The companies were at first administered by the U.S. Navy and were not required to make a profit. Gradually, the companies were phased out and turned over to the local island authorities.

UNITED STATES CONGRESS Since its approval in 1947 of the agreement making nearly all of Micronesia a "strategic trust" of the United States, the U.S. Congress has exercised significant influence over the region by controlling U.S. expenditures for social, economic, and political development terminating the trusteeship. Traditionally, the Senate has allowed the House of Representatives to take the lead in matters concerning Micronesia, but individual members of both houses, from time to time, have also taken a special, if somewhat temporary, interest in the area.

When the administration of the Trust Territory of the Pacific Islands was taken over by the Department of the Interior in 1951, the House and Senate Interior Committees assumed control of the budgetary authorization for the region. Throughout the 1950s, these committees authorized and appropriated less than $6 million annually for administration and development. President John F. Kennedy, and a critical report by a United Nations visiting mission to Micronesia in 1962, pushed the budget to $16 million in 1963. Congress increased this figure gradually each year, then more dramatically, until in 1974 it reached $80 million after which the real-dollar increase tapered off. During the 1960s, major decisions affecting the Trust Territory (q.v.) were made by Wayne Aspinall (Democrat, Colorado), the chairman of the House Committee on Interior and Insular Affairs. Although he permitted increased budget authorizations for Micronesia, Aspinall blocked both administration and congressional initiatives to explore a new political status for the region.

In 1970 younger members of the House Interior Committee succeeded in forcing rule changes to reduce Aspinall's control over his subcommittees. As a result, the chairman of the Subcommittee on Territories, Philip Burton of California, became the dominant congressional force in Micronesian affairs. The creation of a Subcommittee on Pacific Affairs under Antonio Won Pat (q.v.) of Guam did not significantly reduce the jurisdiction of Burton's committee or his control over legislation affecting Micronesia.

In 1975 Burton was instrumental in House passage of a bill approving the establishment of a U.S. Commonwealth of the Northern Mariana Islands (q.v.). The lack of debate in the House contrasted sharply with the Senate where a number of traditionally liberal Senators as well as some conservatives questioned the wisdom of the measure before it passed and was signed into law.

During the 1970s, Burton skillfully shepherded legislation through Congress that provided for larger budgets and expanded federal programs in Micronesia. As negotiations over a new political status for the territory progressed, Burton attempted to introduce provisions that would be required for his support of the final agreement. Yet the Congressional impact on the political status negotiations, as in most issues central to the development of Micronesia, remained limited by the sporadic and poorly informed interests of a few members. In the 1970s, Micronesian leaders moved more confidently to assert their demands for greater political autonomy, and Congress found itself primarily in the role of a spectator to the negotiations.

Through its belated generosity toward Micronesia in the form of increased budgetary and programmatic assistance, Congress intended to improve social and economic conditions in the region. But its lack of sustained interest in Micronesia prevented it from enhancing Micronesian capacities for self-sufficiency.

UNITED STATES AND PACIFIC ISLAND BASES United States-Japanese friction after 1905 presented U.S. military planners with the problem of protecting the Philippines and of supporting U.S. Far Eastern policy. The strategy developed, called War Plan-Orange, emphasized the possession of a string of island bases along which U.S. power could be projected into the Western Pacific. By 1922 Japan's possession of the League of Nations-mandated islands of Micronesia left the key U.S. base, Guam, defenseless in their midst because Washington Naval Treaty prohibited Guam's development as a major base.

The Navy's strategic thinking then centered on the Japanese islands stretching toward Guam and the Philippines, the islands that would screen Hawaii and the Panama Canal, and the islands forming stepping-stones to Australia.

In 1923 a naval vessel was sent on an intelligence cruise through the Japanese islands. Another cruise, jointly sponsored by the Departments of Navy and Agriculture, examined Nihoa, Ocean, Johnston, and Wake. In 1924 a similar expedition visited the islands south of Hawaii: Fanning, Christmas, Jarvis, Washington, Palmyra, Baker, and Howland. The Department of the Navy recommended that the State Department push American claims to Howland, Baker, and Christmas, but the State Department refused to take any action. After 1927 the Navy's interest in the islands waned.

In June 1934, the South Seas Commercial Company (q.v.) approached the Navy with regard to establishing Pacific air routes using Midway, Wake, and Guam for the central route, and Jarvis, Baker, Howland, Johnston, Kingman Reef, and American Samoa for the southwestern route. Ultimately the Navy granted Pan American Airways the permits for the central route while encouraging the South Seas Commercial Company on the other route. By the end of 1934, Japan gave notice that it was abrogating the Naval Treaty of 1922. The Navy could start preparing bases in 1937.

In 1935 naval officers accompanied Pan American's base expedition to Midway and Wake, which they surveyed and plotted for landing fields in the future. In May 1935 patrol planes used Pan American's facilities at Midway during the Navy's war games. In March 1935 the United States colonized Howland, Baker, and Jarvis to establish the United States claim. The first expedition also examined Palmyra, Swain's Island, and Pago Pago; during the second cruise, Johnston was examined; during the third, Kingman Reef was visited along with Palmyra again, due to the Navy's special interest. By the end of 1936, dredging was under way of equal benefit to the Navy. In October, the Navy tried to install deep-sea moorings for patrol planes at Howland. And, at the end of 1936, the Naval Treaty ended.

The Navy started preparing Johnston at the beginning of 1937. In May, a scientific party was carried to Canton Island to observe an eclipse of the sun. The Navy made a complete survey of Howland, which had proved inadequate during the search for missing aviatrix Amelia Earhart. In late July, the Navy wanted to colonize Canton, but the State Department held out for negotiations with Britain. The Department of the Navy did get approval to develop Palmyra and reconsidered trying deep-sea moorings at Howland if Canton could not be obtained. In March 1938 colonists were landed on Canton, and the United States obtained joint use with Pan American, which moved onto the islands, allowing the Navy to use their facilities. In 1939 the Department of the Navy did a complete survey of the Phoenix and Union islands.

The Hepburn report on base needs in December 1938 recommended the development of secondary bases at Midway, Wake, Johnston, Palmyra, Canton, Rose, and Guam. Appropriations were made, but Guam was omitted for fear of upsetting Japan. In late 1939 Navy planes flew to the Philippines through Pan American's central route. The Navy tested Canton in March 1940 and based a flight of patrol planes on Pan American's facilities.

The Greenslade report in January 1941 called for creating main bases at Hawaii and the Philippines to create a balance of power in the Western Pacific. Midway, Wake, and Guam were to be major air bases while Samoa, Johnston, Palmyra, and Canton were to be subsidiary bases to protect Hawaii and the Panama Canal. The Philippines had been upgraded, making it essential that a southwest route to the islands through Australia be set up. In September the Army flew B-17s to the Philippines, using its landing fields at Midway and Wake and then flying to Port Moresby through the Japanese mandated islands. The Moresby leg was dangerous in event of war. The Army sent a construction crew to Canton and one to Christmas late in 1941 and contracted for runways to be built at Suva and at Townsville, Australia, to create a new bomber-ferry route.

On 7 December 1941, only the base at Midway was operational, but Wake, Johnston, and Palmyra ware partly operational and Canton was usable due to Pan American. Wake and Guam, which had never been developed, were taken by Japan. But Midway, Palmyra, Johnston, and Canton were completed, and even Howland and Baker were used. The southwest route to Australia had been established.

UNITED STATES TAKES CONTROL OF GUAM After Guam had been ceded to the United States by the terms of the Treaty of Paris (q.v.), which was signed on 10 December 1898, thus ending the Spanish-American War, the problem for governing the island became a matter of real concern to officials in Washington, D.C. The U.S. Constitution had not provided for the governance of colonies. But President William McKinley, after considering the matter and getting advice from the attorney general, decided to make Guam a naval base.

On 1 January 1899, the coaling ship *Brutus* arrived in Apra Harbor commanded by Lieutenant Vincendon L. Cottman. He appointed Don Jose Sisto, a Spaniard who was the island treasurer, to be acting governor. Cottman also had some unfortunate and disagreeable discussions with Guam's only Chamorro priest, Padre Jose Palomo (q.v.). Consequently, in a report that he submitted on 10 February 1899, Lt. Cottman recommended that, among other things, Washington: (1) expel the priests from Guam, (2) round up the lepers and send them to the Hawaiian island of Molokai, (3) return to Manila all the Filipino convicts, (4) require all males over eighteen to work six days a week, (5) establish compulsory public schools, and (6) make American English the business as well as the official language of Guam.

It appears that before his U.S. departure for Guam, Richard P. Leary (q.v.), Guam's first officially appointed governor, had read and been strongly influenced by Lt. Cottman's report. Upon assuming his official duties on the island, Governor Leary began issuing a series of General Orders. Some of these were readily accepted, while others were deeply resented by the people of Guam. Nevertheless, the General Orders had the effect and force of law and served as the pattern for the Naval Government until 1950. (See Treaty of Paris)

UNIVERSITY OF GUAM The major institution of higher education in the western Pacific, the University of Guam is an accredited five-year, land-grant institution consisting of five colleges, an off-campus program, and a graduate school in which are located three major research units. In 1992 the enrollment was over 3,000.

The university was founded in 1952, when the Guam government established the Territorial College of Guam as a two-year teacher training school within the Department of Education (DOE). The college, which shared facilities with a high school, had an initial enrollment of 190 students and 13 faculty and staff.

In 1960 the college moved to its present 100-acre campus in Mangilao where a two-story classroom building and a library had been erected. In 1963 administrative control was transferred from the DOE to a five-member governing board of regents, and the college was accredited by the Western Association of Schools and Colleges as a four-year degree-granting institution.

In 1968 the college was renamed the University of Guam. Enrollment was 1,800 with a faculty and staff of over 130. Additions to the physical plant have been continued over the years. Major construction programs were undertaken in 1970 and again in 1990.

Administrative autonomy was granted in 1976 with its establishment as a nonmembership, nonprofit corporation under the governance, control, and operation of a Board of Regents. (See Guam, University of)

URDANETA, FRAY ANDRES (1498–?) One of the most important figures in Guam's early history, Urdaneta was born in Villafranca, Spain, in 1498. As a young Spanish military man he distinguished himself in wars in Germany and Italy, and afterwards became an outstanding student of mathematics and astronomy. This led him to navigation, and in 1526 he came to Guam with the expedition commanded by Fray Garcia Jofre de Loaisa. After a stay of only four days, the expedition pushed on to the Moluccas, where they remained for some ten years before getting back to Spain in 1536. Not long after this, perhaps as a result of his adventures at sea, Urdaneta went to Mexico, and after some years of study, made his profession as a priest in the Augustinian Order.

Yet, because he was such a capable navigator, he was selected to accompany the Philippine-bound expedition of Miguel Lopez de Legazpi (q.v.) as pilot. They arrived at Guam on 22 January 1565, and four days later on 26 January the group went ashore where Legazpi formally claimed the island for Spain, after which Father Urdaneta celebrated what might have been the first mass in the Marianas; certainly it was the first documented mass.

The party stayed for eleven days and then went on to the Philippines to establish Spanish claims there. After this, Father Urdaneta navigated the flagship *San Pablo* (q.v.) northward toward Japan and then across the vast Pacific via the Japanese current to lower California some 130 days later. A few days after this, the group reached the tranquil waters of Acapulco Harbor. It was due to the navigational skills of Padre Urdaneta that the return route from the Philippines to America had been found at last.

V

VILLALOBOS, FRANCISCO RAMON DE Villalobos was governor of Guam from 1831–1837. A dedicated, energetic governor, Villalobos was first sent to Guam in 1828 to look into conditions on the island. His investigation and report led to the removal of Governor Medinilla and to his own appointment as governor in 1831.

Villalobos expanded agricultural production, drained swampland, and introduced new crops such as coffee. He initiated fiscal reforms, especially those regarding port fees and import duties. He also oversaw the construction of new bridges and roads and the repair of public buildings. He wrote a memoir of the Mariana islands in 1833.

W

WAR CRIMES TRIALS United States Naval authorities supervised the war crimes trials in the Pacific Islands. Massive investigations were launched to collect evidence in the

Mariana, Gilbert, Caroline, and Bonin islands. In all, there were forty-seven trials held from 1945 to 1949, three on Kwajalein and forty-four on Guam, the administrative headquarters for the program. During the trials, 127 Japanese, 12 Saipanese, 2 Rotanese, 2 Guamanians, and 1 Palauan were tried. One hundred and thirteen were convicted and fourteen executed (all fourteen were Japanese military personnel). Some of the convictions stemmed from the killing of downed airmen, fatal medical experiments on prisoners of war, and cannibalism (q.v.). One of the trials involved the mass execution of ninety-eight Pan American Airways civilian employees on Wake Island in 1943.

WAR OF JENKIN'S EAR This was a struggle that Britain got into in order to gain trade access to Spain's American and West Indian ports in the 1740s. This war was named after the British sea captain who inflamed public opinion with tales of how the Spanish had cut off one of his ears.

The War of Jenkin's Ear touched Micronesia when Commodore George Anson (q.v.) came to the western Pacific to capture Spanish galleon treasure to help pay the British costs for the war. In his ship *Centurion,* Anson crossed the Pacific toward Manila after missing the eastbound galleon at Acapulco. His aim was to capture the westbound galleon, which carried great amounts of treasure. He had three other ships besides the *Centurion:* the *Gloucester,* the *Tyral,* and the *Severn.* Only the *Centurion* survived Anson's Pacific exploits.

In Micronesia, Anson stopped at Tinian in the Marianas to rest and recuperate. He next stopped at Guam before proceeding to Manila in May 1742, where he encountered and captured the great galleon *Nuestra Senora de Cavadonga* in a fierce battle in the San Bernardino Straits.

Returning to England with his treasure, Anson was heralded and immediately promoted to rear admiral. Later he was made First Lord of the Admiralty, Britain's highest-ranking naval officer.

WASHINGTON NAVAL CONFERENCE The Washington Disarmament Conference of 1922 is also referred to as the

Washington Naval Conference. The conference was sponsored by the United States and sought to solve the problems of the naval armaments race and the open-door policy toward China and the Far East. Among a number of provisions signed were three interconnected ones that temporarily eased the tensions between Japan and the United States. The five-power treaty that was signed created a naval tonnage ratio system for five nations, including Japan and the U.S. Japan agreed to accept a lesser tonnage, 60 percent of naval ships, in return for the U.S. stopping all military base construction west of Hawaii. This left Japan dominant in the western Pacific.

For Guam, this naval conference resulted in the actual removal of some armaments. It also created a problem for growth on Guam, since any development of port facilities and harbors could be construed as military buildup. All through this period, the U.S. kept to its part of the bargain, although it is not clear that Japan did. Japan also had a fleet that could project itself all over the Pacific since the distance from Japan into the west and south Pacific is not as great as it is for the U.S. fleet coming all the way from California.

When war finally came to Guam in December 1941, the defense consisted of only a scant garrison of Marines and the Guam Insular Force. The Japanese made a swift and humiliating capture of the island.

WESTERN IMPERIALISM The twentieth century concept of colonialism as a moral evil that should be eradicated represents a response to the colonial-imperial situations of the past three centuries in Oceania. The Pacific islands, which Europeans colonized between the sixteenth and nineteenth centuries, gained self-government or independence by the twentieth-century post-World War II period. The major European colonial powers of Spain, France, Germany, Great Britain, and the United States are all advanced capitalist nations, and with the exception of Spain whose colonial motivations were religious, all employed economic arguments in the advocacy of their expansionist views and political imposition on the fragile cultures of the Pacific.

Historian Oskar H. K. Spate has pointed out that by the middle of the sixteenth century the Pacific Ocean was referred to correctly as a "Spanish lake." After Balboa's discovery of the "South Sea," Spain gradually extended her domination along nearly the whole eastern rim of the Pacific. Then, starting with Magellan's voyage, Spain explored the possibility of reaching the coveted Moluccas (Spice Islands) by crossing the ocean. After the discovery of the return route from the western Pacific to the Americas in 1565, Spain established her domination over the Philippines and later over Micronesia. This enabled Spain to gain a share in the wealth of Asia through the Manila Galleon (q.v.) trade, which proceeded uninterruptedly until 1815 when she lost her American colonies. Spanish expeditions in the south Pacific resulted in discovery of some islands of Melanesia and Polynesia. Finally, Spain also took part in the last phase of Pacific exploration starting in the eighteenth century with the voyages of the navigator Malaspina. He and the scientists who accompanied him collected data that filled many volumes. Spain remained present in the ocean until the end of the nineteenth century when serious revolts occurred in the Philippines and the Spanish-American War broke out, which resulted in her losing the Philippines and Guam to the United States in 1898.

France, compared with other European powers who played major roles in the Pacific, entered the region comparatively late. Official French support for Pacific navigation came after the Seven Years War of 1756–1763, and there had been by that time over 100 Frenchmen who had circumnavigated the globe. Louis Antoine de Bouganville took possession of Tahiti, Samoa, Vanuatu, the Solomons, and New Ireland. Other important French Pacific explorers were Etienne Marchand, Antoine d'Entrecasteaux, Jean-Francois de Laperouse, Louise de Freycinet (q.v.), Louis Duperrey (q.v.), and Dumont d'Urville (q.v.). By the end of the nineteenth century, France had annexed the Society Islands, the Tuamotus, the Marquesas, the Australs, the Gambiers, and New Caledonia, and had entered into a condominium agreement with Great Britain over the control of Vanuatu (New Hebrides).

The Germans also came late into the Pacific through the presence, in 1857, of the trading firm of J. C. Godeffroy und

Sohn (q.v.), which established a station at Samoa. They flew the flag of the ancient Hansa city of Hamburg, since a German nation-state did not exist until 1870. Godeffroy and other German companies expanded to Tonga, the Marshalls and Carolines, and to New Guinea. They exported copra (q.v.), cotton, and pearl shell amounting to over 5 million marks annually. In 1884 Chancellor Bismarck annexed the islands as colonies and awarded administering charters to various companies. From the mid-1880s to 1914, Germany enjoyed the greatest commercial weight in the islands. In Micronesia, Spain contested Germany's claims to the Carolines, but finally sold all her Micronesian possessions to the Germans after the Spanish-American War in 1898. Germany's colonies were taken over within weeks of the declaration of war in August 1914: Samoa by a New Zealand expeditionary force, Micronesia by the Japanese, and New Guinea by Australian troops after token encounters.

The growth of the British Empire in the Pacific was characterized by maximum acquisition with minimum enthusiasm. Great Britain had taken Manila in 1762, Tahiti in 1767, and the continent of Australia in 1770, but it was only the latter that stuck after England decided to locate convicts there in 1787 following the loss of her American colonies. In 1840 New Zealand was annexed and missionized; Fiji was treated likewise in 1874. The large colonies of Australia and New Zealand pushed for their control of other island groups such as the Cook Islands, parts of New Guinea, Samoa, the Solomons, and Vanuatu.

The United States entered the Pacific shortly after the American Revolution in search of trade with Asia. Between 1778 and the 1830s, Americans came to dominate the northwest Pacific fur trade, and visited Japan, Polynesia, and the coast of South America. Other Pacific Ocean areas were also visited by American ships that were searching for sandalwood, *bêche-de-mer* (q.v.), and shells for trade on the rimlands. Yet, the effects of American presence were more important for the lives of the Pacific islanders than for the U.S. economy. In the nineteenth century, whaling (q.v.) became an important economic activity for the United States. American crews helped introduce disease germs, firearms, alcohol (q.v.), and violence as well as new materials, tools, technologies, plants, and ideas including Christianity. Protestant missionaries from Hawaii extended their teachings to the Marquesas, Marshalls, and Carolines. In the middle of the nineteenth century a search for soil-enriching fertilizers prompted the passage of the Guano Act by Congress in 1856. This act enabled Americans to claim for the government any unclaimed islands in the Pacific, which could be mined for guano deposits or phosphate. U.S. Naval vessels were sent to the Pacific early in the nineteenth century to protect and police the Americans pursuing their various interests there. A Pacific squadron, based on the South American coast, often sent ships to the Pacific after 1821. Other American ships from the Asiatic squadron, based at Hong Kong, carried out missions in cooperation with consular agents. From 1838 to 1842, Lieutenant Charles Wilkes led a navy-exploring expedition through the eastern Pacific, and later in the 1840s a similar expedition charted the Sea of Japan. In the 1890s, the U.S. acquired Hawaii, Samoa, Midway, Wake, Guam, and the Philippines.

By the twentieth century, the United States, with a history of anticolonial sentiment, had become a colonial power in the Pacific without a colonial office, trained colonial officials, or any real model for colonial administration except that provided by the history of the continental territories destined for statehood with the American union. Because of their relationship to military security problems, the Philippines were placed under the jurisdiction of the War Department, while Guam and American Samoa were given to the Navy to administer. Only Hawaii was set on a normal territorial path toward statehood.

Altruism and humanitarianism combined with the economic and political factors that contributed to the European and American expansion in the Pacific over the 393 years from 1521 to 1914. Undesirable cultural practices such as cannibalism, infanticide, and human sacrifice were obliterated along with much important cultural and societal information. Many colonials sincerely desired to eliminate tribal warfare; to establish law and order; to introduce Christianity and western education, including modern science and technology; and to raise living standards by promoting trade and commerce. But they tended to justify their benevolence on the basis of concepts like ''The White Man's Burden'' the *mission civilisatrice,* Social Darwinism, and pseudoscientific racist theories that regarded Pacific islanders as biologically or culturally inferior to white people. As a result, Western colonialism involved not only domination and exploitation, but also humiliation of island peoples. The legacy of this situation is a reaction against discrimination and feelings of inferiority on the part of islanders, especially after many of them had come to accept Western ideals about human dignity, freedom, and equality, and Western ideas about the rights of men and of nations.

WHALING In North America and Europe during the eighteenth and nineteenth centuries, the oil of whales, particularly sperm whales, was in great demand for candles. In addition, their bones were used for women's corsets and other manufactured products.

   Whaling was begun in Micronesia by British ships in the 1820s. Between 1840 and 1860, great numbers of whale ships, mostly American vessels by this time, put in at Pohnpei, Kosrae, Saipan, and Guam for stopovers that lasted from a few days to several weeks. While the ships took on fresh water, wood, and provisions, the crew enjoyed themselves ashore. Many sailors grew so fond of life on a tropical island that they deserted. Ships captains often recruited islanders to fill out the ship's complement. As well as allowing some young island men to see the world, whaling brought Western goods to Micronesia. Tobacco, muskets, iron items, and clothing were traded for pigs, yams, and taro. Petrolem, which was discovered in Pennsylvania in 1859, began to replace whale oil as a fuel to light homes. For this and other reasons, whaling declined rapidly in the 1860s. As late as 1903, however, a lone whaler could be seen riding at anchor in Guam's Apra Harbor.

WON PAT, ANTONIO BORJA (1908–1987) Won Pat was a Guam educator, businessman, and politician. Born in Sumay and educated in Guam's schools, Won Pat taught school from 1926 until the Japanese invasion in 1941. He was elected to the Guam Congress (q.v.) in 1936. He returned to teaching following the war and re-entered politics in 1948, being elected speaker of the Guam Congress's House of Assembly. He was speaker of the First, Second, Fourth, Fifth, Sixth, and Seventh legislatures (q.v.). He was elected Guam's first Washington Representative (1965–1972) and first delegate to the United States Congress (1972–1984). Won Pat was one of the principal architects of the Organic Act (q.v.) of Guam. He was responsible for many federally funded capital improvement projects related to highways and roads, water, power, health, and education.

WORLD WAR II (See Duenas, Jesus Baza; Eniwetok, Battle of, 1944; *Enola Gay*; Gilbert Islands, Battle of, 1943; Great Marianas Turkey Shoot; Guam Liberation in World War II; Kwajalein, Battle of, 1944; Makin, Raid on, 1942; McMillin, George J.; Nimitz, Chester W.; Peleliu, Battle of, 1944; Saipan, Battle of, 1944; Tinian, Battle of, 1944; Truk (Chuuk), Reduction of, 1944; Tweed, George Ray; War Crimes Trials in Micronesia; Yokoi, Shoichi)

WORLD WAR II IN MICRONESIA The Central Pacific campaign of World War II, led by Admiral Chester W. Nimitz (q.v.), affected Micronesia greatly. In the islands, military-sector materiel, facilities, and manpower began to be organized after Japan withdrew from the League of Nations in 1935. Actual fortifications were begun, however, only after the outbreak of hostilities in 1941 at Pearl Harbor, Hawaii. In November 1943, Americans invaded the Gilbert Islands (q.v.) at Tarawa, while other Allied forces of Americans and Australians under the overall command of General Douglas MacArthur, invaded New Guinea at Rabaul. The American capture of the formidable base at Kwajelien (q.v.) in the Marshall Islands showed the disadvantage of those islands, which the Japanese Navy had regarded as "unsinkable aircraft carriers." After Admiral Nimitz captured Majuro in the Marshalls, he was able to move his base headquarters from Pearl Harbor, Hawaii, and position himself 2,000 miles farther west and closer to the Japanese home islands.

The next objective in the Central Pacific Campaign was the Marianas. Truk (Chuuk), in the Carolines, was known as the "Gibraltar of the Pacific," but was effectively neutralized from the American bases in the Marshall Islands. Heavy and successful air raids were implemented in February 1944, while at the same time, Eniwetok (q.v.) in the Marshalls was captured. The successive raids on Truk (q.v.) led by Admiral Marc Mitscher's Task Force 58 of fast carriers destroyed more than 210 aircraft and 200,000 tons of shipping at the American cost of one carrier damaged and seventeen aircraft shot down.

The Marianas were the very center of Japan's network of airfields on which their outer defenses depended. Nimitz's assault on the Marianas brought out the Japanese Imperial Combined Fleet to fight. This fleet was led by Admiral Toyoda Soemu, since Admiral Koga Mineichi had been killed in an air crash in March 1944 when the Americans bombed Palau.

The attack on the Marianas began on 12 June 1944 with a predawn strike. Two Marine divisions and one Army division were used for the main landings at Saipan (q.v.) on 15 June. The Combined Fleet had time to concentrate because Admiral Toyoda had expected an attack on the Carolines. He had to intervene, and he attacked on 19 June with nine carriers against the fifteen of the American force. His inexperienced pilots were no match for the Americans, and more than 300 Japanese aircraft were lost in what has come to be known as the "great Marianas turkey shoot," (q.v.) while the Americans lost only eighteen fighters and twelve bombers. This overall engagement was known as the Battle of the Philippine Sea. While the Japanese aircraft losses were great, the Japanese Combined Fleet was not destroyed. Only three Japanese carriers were sunk, so the Japanese force, although considerably weakened, remained in existence.

Nimitz struck next at Palau with the Battle of Peleliu (q.v.) in September 1944. It was a bloody engagement and little was known about the terrain of the island in which the Japanese had dug in with a system of cave defenses containing some 300 fortresses. In the larger caves electric lighting, ventilation, telephones, stairs, and radios had been installed.

Over 6,000 American casualties including killed and wounded, were counted.

With Marianas bases at Guam, Tinian, and Saipan, and with Palau and the Marshalls secured and occupied while the Carolines were neutralized and allowed to "die on the vine," the Pacific war in Micronesia was over, although the wider war was not won until August 1945 after the American B-29 *Enola Gay* (q.v.), flying from Tinian (q.v.), dropped atomic bombs on Hiroshima and Nagasaki. The formal surrender was signed aboard the *USS Missouri* in Tokyo Bay on 1 September 1945.

Subsequent to the war in Micronesia, a series of war crimes trials (q.v.) were held at Guam, which resulted in convictions, incarcerations, and some executions for Japanese officers. During the years following World War II in Micronesia, a number of Japanese "stragglers" were discovered, the most famous being Yokoi Shoichi (q.v.), who was discovered at Guam in 1972. (See Duenas, Jesus Baza; Guam Liberation in World War II; Makin, Raid on, 1942; McMillin, George J.; Tweed, George Ray)

Y

YANAIHARA, TADAO (1893–1961) A Japanese colonial theorist, professor, and scholar who developed the idea of colonial trusteeship for Japan in the British and American sense. He wrote extensively on Micronesia. He was a student at Tokyo University, of Nitobe Inazo, who was called away to participate in the League of Nations deliberations on colonialism. Yanaihara then collated and edited Nitobe's lectures on colonialism and eventually assumed Nitobe's chair in colonial policy at the university in 1937. A Christian, Yanaihara surpassed eventually the contributions to Japanese colonial theory by Nitobe. He focused on both detailed institutional studies and broad theoretical problems of colonialism.

In institutional terms, Yanaihara minutely examined the mechanisms of colonial administration not only of Japan but of other colonial systems, devoting particular attention to comparing and contrasting Japan's position in Taiwan and Korea with Britain's imperial policies in Canada and Ireland. On a broader plan, Yanaihara's interests dealt with imperialism as a theory and with its particular function in the Japanese case.

His perspective was economic, and his interests ranged in the entire spectrum of economic, political and social problems in the Japanese empire, and his research, supported by extensive travel and observation, each and all of Japan's colonial territories. (See Japan in Micronesia)

YAP CRISIS See Japan in Micronesia

YAPESE STONE MONEY Yapese stone money, called *rai,* is unique to Yap in the Caroline Islands. These huge aragonite disks were fashioned by hand in quarries in Palau and then transported over 300 miles of open ocean to Yap. In return for being able to quarry the stone in Palau, the Yapese provided services such as fortune-telling and shaman healing. The largest existing piece of *rai* is over twelve feet in diameter. The largest piece known was quarried in the late 1890s and brought to Yap abroad the ship of David Dean ''His Majesty'' O'Keefe (q.v.), who had set up a trade monopoly in copra (q.v.) with the Yapese in return for transporting their money; the piece, however, slipped overboard while being transferred to a smaller craft in Yap Harbor. The last known piece to be fashioned was made during the early Japanese administration (1914–1944). (See *Udoud*)

YOKOI, SHOICHI (1912–) Yokoi was a noncommissioned officer in the Imperial Japanese Army during World War II. In July 1944, he was stationed on Guam when the island was recaptured by American forces. Rather than surrender, Yokoi, along with many of his comrades, went into hiding. Over the years these stragglers were captured, surrendered, or died. Yokoi was the last to hold out, being discovered in the Talofofo area in January 1972. He later ran, unsuccessfully, for elective office in Japan. A book was written about his twenty-eight years in the jungles of Guam.

INTRODUCTION TO SELECTED
BIBLIOGRAPHY

The following bibliography does not pretend to be a comprehensive one. Rather we have stressed works on the history and cultures of the region, and those on modern social, cultural, and political change. We have divided the entries into the following categories:

Bibliography
Culture
Description and Travel
Education
History
History—World War II
Language
Politics and Government
Reference
Religion
Society

We have included an extensive "Description and Travel" section since these firsthand accounts of the islands are usually of great interest to readers from outside the region. The approach of numerous fiftieth anniversaries of Second World War events led us to compile a special subdivision focusing on the war.

Many of the books and articles cited are available in American libraries, or are easily obtained through interlibrary loan. Materials produced within Micronesia, however, are generally not found in North American libraries. The two best sources for these items are the Pacific Collection at Hamilton Library, University of Hawaii, and the Pacific Collection of the Micronesian Area Research Center, University of Guam.

SELECTED BIBLIOGRAPHY

BIBLIOGRAPHY

Coppell, William G. and S. Stratigos. *A Bibliography of Pacific Island Theses and Dissertations.* Honolulu: University of Hawaii Press, 1983.

Goetzfridt, Nicholas J. and William L. Wuerch. *Micronesia 1975–1987: A Social Science Bibliography.* New York: Greenwood Press, 1989.

Hatanaka, Sachiko. *A Bibliography of Micronesia Compiled from Japanese Publications, 1915–1945.* Occasional Papers, 8. Tokyo: Gakushuin University, Research Institute for Oriental Cultures, 1979.

Jackson, Miles M., ed. *Pacific Islands Studies: A Survey of the Literature.* New York: Greenwood Press, 1986.

Marshall, Mac, and James D. Nason. *Micronesia 1944–1974: A Bibliography of Anthropological and Related Source Materials.* New Haven, CT: Human Relations Area File Press, 1975.

Trussel, Stephen. *Gilbertese Bibliography: Lists and Indexes of Works Pertaining to the Gilbert Islands.* Honolulu: University of Hawaii, Linguistics Department, 1978.

Utinomi, Huzio. *Bibliography of Micronesia.* Honolulu: University of Hawaii, 1952.

CULTURE

Alden, John E. "A Press in Paradise: The Beginnings of Printing in Micronesia" *The Papers of the Bibliographical Society of America* 38 (1944), pp. 269–283.

Alkire, William H. *An Introduction to the Peoples and Cultures of Micronesia.* Menlo Park, CA: Cummings, 1977.

Ashby, Gene, ed. *Never and Always: Micronesian Stories of the Origins of Islands, Landmarks, and Customs.* Eugene, OR: Rainy Day Press, 1983.

———. *Ponape: An Island Argosy.* Eugene, OR: Rainy Day Press, 1983.

———, ed. *Some Things of Value: Micronesian Customs as Seen by Micronesians.* Eugene, OR: Rainy Day Press, 1981.

Athens, J. Stephen. "The Megalithic Ruins of Nan Madol: Archaeology and Oral History Join Forces on a Pacific Island." *Natural History* 92, 2 (1983), pp. 50–61.

Barnett, H. G. *Being a Palauan.* New York: Holt, 1959.

Brower, Kenneth. *Micronesia: The Land, the People, and the Sea.* Baton Rouge, LA: Louisiana State University Press, 1981.

Bryan, E. H., Jr. *Life in the Marshall Islands.* Honolulu: Bishop Museum, 1972.

Christian, F. W. *The Caroline Islands: Travel in the Sea of Little Islands.* London: Methuen, 1899.

Colletta, Nat J. *American Schools for the Natives of Ponape: A Study of Education and Culture Change in Micronesia.* Honolulu: University of Hawaii Press, 1980.

Ellis, William S., and James P. Blair. "A Way of Life Lost: Bikini." *National Geographic* 169, 6 (1986), pp. 813–834.

Fensham, Florence A., and Buelah Logan Tuthill. *The Old and the New in Micronesia.* Chicago: Women's Board of Missions of the Interior, 1907.

Fischer, John L. *The Eastern Carolines.* New Haven, CT: Human Relations Area Files Press, 1970.

Force, Roland W. *Leadership and Cultural Change in Palau.* Fieldiana: Anthropology, 50. Chicago: Natural History Museum, 1960.

Fritz, Georg. *The Chamorros: A History and Ethnography of the Mariana Islands,* trans. E. Craddock. Mangilao, Guam: University of Guam, Micronesian Area Research Center, 1984.

———. *The Chamorro: A History and Ethnography of the Marianas,* trans. Elfriede Craddock. Saipan: Division of Historic Preservation, 1989.

Gladwin, Thomas. *East is a Big Bird: Navigation and Logic on Puluwat Atoll.* Cambridge, MA: Harvard University Press, 1970.

———, and Seymour B. Sarason. *Truk: Man in Paradise.* Viking Fund Publications in Anthropology, 20. New York: Wenner-Gren Foundation for Anthropological Research, 1953.

Goodenough, Ward H. *Property, Kin, and Community in Truk.* Hamden, CT: Archon Books, 1978.

Grey, Eve. *Legends of Micronesia.* Saipan: Trust Territory Department of Education, 1951.

Grimble, Arthur. *Migrations, Myth and Magic from the Gilbert Islands.* London: Routledge and Paul, 1972.

———. *A Pattern of Islands.* London: Murray, 1952.

———. *Return to the Islands: Life and Legend in the Gilberts.* London: Murray, 1947.

———. *We Chose the Islands: A Six-Year Adventure in the Gilberts.* New York: Morrow, 1952.

Hezel, Francis X. "From Conversion to Conquest: The Early Spanish Mission in the Marianas." *Journal of Pacific History* 17, 3 (1982), pp. 115–137.

Hidikata, H. *Stone Images of Palau.* Mangilao, Guam: University of Guam, Micronesian Area Research Center, 1973.

Johannes, R. E. *Words of the Lagoon: Fishing and Marine Lore in the Palau District of Micronesia.* Berkeley: University of California Press, 1981.

Joseph, Alice, and Veronica Murray. *Chamorros and Carolinians of Saipan.* Cambridge, MA: Harvard University Press, 1951.

Kubary, Johann Stanislaus. "Die Palau-Inseln in der Sudsee." *Journal des Museum Godeffroy* 1 (1873), pp. 177–238.

———. "Uber des Einheimische Geld auf der Insel Yap und auf den Palau Inseln." *In Ethnographische Beitrage zur Kenntnis des Karolinen Archipels.* Leiden: van der Hoek, 1889.

Lessa, William A. *Drake's Island of Thieves: Ethnological Sleuthing.* Honolulu: University Press of Hawaii, 1975.

———. "An Evaluation of Early Descriptions of Carolinian Culture." *Ethnohistory* 9 (1962), pp. 313–403.

———. *Tales from Ulithi Atoll: A Comparative Study in Oceanic Folklore.* Folklore Studies, 13. Berkeley: University of California Press, 1961.

Lewis, David. *We, the Navigators.* Wellington: Reed, 1972.

Lingenfelter, Richard E. *Presses of the Pacific Islands, 1817–1867.* Los Angeles: Plantin Press, 1967.

Lingenfelter, Sherwood G. *Yap: Political Leadership and Culture Change in an Island Society.* Honolulu: University of Hawaii Press, 1975.

Lundsgaarde, Henry P. *Cultural Adaptation in the Southern Gilbert Islands.* Eugene: University of Oregon, 1966.

Marshall, Mac. *Weekend Warriors: Alcohol in a Micronesian Culture.* Palo Alto: Mayfield Publishing Co., 1979.

————, and Leslie Marshall. "Holy and Unholy Spirits," *Journal of Pacific History* 11 (1976), pp. 135–166.

Mason, Leonard, ed., *Kiribati: A Changing Atoll Culture.* Suva, Fiji: University of the South Pacific, Institute of Pacific Studies, 1985.

Maude, Henry E. *The Evolution of Gilbertese Boti: An Ethnohistorical Interpretation.* Suva, Fiji: University of the South Pacific, Institute of Pacific Studies, 1977.

Osborne, Douglas. *The Archeology of the Palau Islands: An Intensive Study.* Honolulu: Bishop Museum, 1966.

Parmentier, Richard J. *The Sacred Remains: Myth, History, and Polity in Belau.* Chicago: University of Chicago Press, 1987.

Paszkowski, Lech. "John Stanislaw Kubary—Naturalist and Ethnographer of the Pacific Islands." *Australian Zoologist* 16 (1971), pp. 43–70.

Petersen, Glenn T. *One Man Cannot Rule a Thousand: Fission in a Ponapean Chiefdom.* Ann Arbor, MI: University of Michigan Press, 1982.

Phelan, Nancy. *Atoll Holiday.* Sydney, Australia: Angus & Robertson, 1958.

Poyer, Linette. "The Ngatik Massacre: Documentary and Oral Traditional Accounts." *Journal of Pacific History* 20, 1 (1985), pp. 4–22.

Reed, Erik K. *Archaeology and History of Guam.* Washington, DC: National Park Service, 1952.

Safford, William Edwin. *The Useful Plants of Guam, with an Introductory Account of the Physical Features and Natural History of the Island, of the Character and History of its People, and of their Agriculture.* Washington, DC: National Museum, 1905.

Semper, K. *The Palau Islands in the Pacific.* trans. Mark L. Berg. Guam: University of Guam, Micronesian Area Research Center, 1982.

Spoehr, Alexander. *Majuro: A Village in the Marshall Islands.* Fieldiana: Anthropology, 39. Chicago: Natural History Museum, 1949.

———. *Marianas Prehistory: Archaeological Survey and Excavations on Saipan, Tinian, and Rota.* Chicago: Natural History Museum, 1957.

———. *Saipan: The Ethnology of a War-Devastated Island.* Fieldiana: Anthropology, 39. Chicago: Natural History Museum, 1954.

Thompson, Laura M. *Guam and Its People: A Study of Cultural Change and Colonial Education.* Princeton: Princeton University Press, 1947.

———. *The Native Culture of the Mariana Islands.* Bishop Museum Bulletin, 185. Honolulu: Bishop Museum, 1945.

Trumbull, Robert. *Tin Roofs and Palm Trees: A Report on the*

New South Seas. Seattle and London: University of Washington Press, 1977.

Van Peenan, M. *Chamorro Legends of the Island of Guam.* Guam: University of Guam, Micronesian Area Research Center, 1974.

Wenkam, Robert, and Byron Baker. *Micronesia—The Breadfruit Revolution.* Honolulu: East-West Center, 1971.

Wright, Cliff. *Christ and Kiribati Culture.* Kiribati: Protestant Church, 1981.

DESCRIPTION AND TRAVEL

Arago, Jacques. *Narrative of a Voyage Round the World, in the Uranie and Physicienne corvettes, commanded by Captain Freycinet, during the years 1817, 1818, 1819, and 1820.* Bibliotheca Australiana, 45. New York: Da Capo, 1971.

Blair, E. H. and J. A. Robertson, eds. *The Philippine Islands.* Cleveland, OH: Arthur H. Clark, 1906.

Bliss, Theodora Crosby. *Micronesia: Fifty Years in the Island World.* Boston: ABCFM, 1906.

Bridge, Cyprian. *Some Recollections.* London: John Murray, 1918.

Brower, Kenneth. *Micronesia: The Land, the People, and the Sea.* Baton Rouge, LA: Louisiana State University Press, 1981.

Bryan, E. H., Jr. *Life in the Marshall Islands.* Honolulu: Bishop Museum, 1972.

Burney, James. *A Chronological History of the Voyages and Discoveries in the South Sea or Pacific Ocean. Vol. V.* Bibliotheca Australiana, 7. New York: Da Capo, 1967.

Chamisso, Adelbert von. *A Voyage Around the World with the Romanzov Exploring Expedition in the Years 1815–1818 in the Brig Rurik, Captain Otto von Kotzebue,* trans. and ed. Henry Kratz. Honolulu: University of Hawaii Press, 1986.

Cheyne, Andrew. *A Description of Some Islands in the Western Pacific Ocean, North and South of the Equator; with Sailing Directions.* London: J. D. Potter, 1852.

———. *The Trading Voyages of Andrew Cheyne.* ed. Dorothy Shineberg. Pacific History Series, 3. Canberra: Australian National University Press, 1971.

Christian, F. W. *The Caroline Islands: Travel in the Sea of Little Islands.* London: Methuen, 1899.

Coontz, Robert E. *From the Mississippi to the Sea.* Philadelphia: Dorrance, 1930.

Coulter, John Wesley. *The Pacific Mandates of the United States.* New York: Macmillan, 1957.

Cox, L. M. *The Island of Guam.* Washington, DC: Government Printing Office, 1917.

Crawford, David and Leona Crawford. *Missionary Adventures in the South Pacific.* Rutland, VT and Tokyo: Charles E. Tuttle, 1967.

Dampier, William. *A New Voyage Round the World.* London: Adam and Charles Black, 1937.

Dana, Julian. *Gods Who Die: The Story of Samoa's Greatest Adventurer.* New York: Macmillan, 1935.

Delano, Amasa. *A Narrative of Voyages and Travels in the Northern and Southern Hemispheres.* Boston: E. G. House, 1817.

Dewar, J. Cumming. *The Voyage of the "Nyanza," R. N. Y. C., Being the Record of a Three Years' Cruise in a Schooner Yacht in the Atlantic and Pacific and Her Subsequent Shipwreck.* Edinburgh and London: William Blackwood and Sons, 1892.

Driver, Marjorie G. *Fray Juan Probe de Zamora and His Account of the Mariana Islands, 1602.* Mangilao, Guam: University of Guam, Micronesian Area Research Center, 1983.

Ellis, Albert. *Ocean Island and Nauru: Their Story.* Sydney: Angus and Robertson, 1935.

Ellis, Williams S., and James P. Blair. "A Way of Life Lost: Bikini." *National Geographic* 169, 6 (1986), pp. 813–834.

Emerson, Rupert, et al. *America's Pacific Dependencies.* New York: American Institute of Pacific Relations, 1949.

Fahey, James J. *Pacific War Diary.* New York: Avon Books, 1963.

Fensham, Florence A., and Beulah Logan Tuthill. *The Old and the New in Micronesia.* Chicago: Women's Board of Missions of the Interior, 1907.

Fischer, John L. *The Eastern Carolines.* New Haven, CT: Human Relations Area Files Press, 1970.

Freycinet, Louis de. *Voyage autour du monde . . . execute sur les corvettes de S.M. l'Uranie e la Physicienne, pendant les annees 1817, 1818, 1819, et 1820.* Paris: Pillet Aine, 1829.

Furness, William Henry. *The Island of Stone Money: Uap of the Carolines.* Philadelphia and London: Lippincott, 1910.

Geographic, Military, and Political Description of the Island of Guam. Francisco Ramon de Villalobos, trans. Felicia Plaza. MARC Working Papers, 8. Mangilao, Guam: University of Guam, Micronesian Area Research Center, 1969.

Gilbert, Thomas. *A Voyage from New South Wales to Canton in the Year 1788.* London: Debrett, 1789.

Goerner, Fred G. *The Search for Amelia Earhart.* Garden City, NY: Doubleday, 1966.

Grimble, Arthur. *A Pattern of Islands.* London: Murray, 1952.

————. *Return to the Islands: Life and Legend in the Gilberts.* London: Murray, 1947.

————. *We Chose the Islands: A Six-Year Adventure in the Gilberts.* New York: Morrow, 1952.

Gulick, Luther H. "Lectures on Micronesia," *52nd Annual Report of the Hawaiian Historical Society.* Honolulu: Hawaiian Historical Society, 1943.

Haswell, William. "Remarks on a Voyage in 1801 to the Island of Guam." *Historical Collections of the Essex Institute* 53, 3 (1917), pp. 193–214.

Hockin, John P. *A Supplement to the Account of the Pelew Islands; Compiled from the Journals of the 'Panther' and 'Endeavour,' Two Vessels sent by the Honourable East India Company to those Islands in the Year 1790.* London: G & W Nicol, 1803.

Holden, Horace. *A Narrative of the Shipwreck, Captivity and Sufferings of Horace Holden and Benjamin H. Nute; who were Cast away in the American Ship 'Mentor,' on the Pelew Islands, in the Year 1832.* Boston: Russell, Shattuck, 1836.

Ibanez, A. *Chronicles of the Mariana Islands,* trans. Marjorie G. Driver. Mangilao, Guam: University of Guam, Micronesian Area Research Center, 1974.

Ibanez del Carmen, Aniceto, and Francisco et al Resano. *Chronical of the Mariana Islands,* trans. Marjorie D. Driver. Guam:

University of Guam, Micronesia Area Research Center, 1976.

Ibanez y Garcia, Luis de. *History of the Mariana, Caroline, and Palau Islands.* MARC Educational Series, 12. Mangilao, Guam: University of Guam, Micronesian Area Research Center, 1992.

Keate, Geroge. *An Account of the Pelew Islands, situated in the Western Part of the Pacific Ocean, Composed from the Journals and Communications of Captain Henry Wilson, and Some of His Officers, who, in August 1783, Were Shipwrecked in the Antelope . . .* London: G. Nicol, 1789.

Kotzebue, Otto von. *A New Voyage Round the World in the Years 1823, 24, 25 and 26.* London: Colburn and Bently, 1830.

———. *A Voyage of Discovery into the South Sea and Bering's Straits . . . in the Years 1815–1818.* London: Longman and Brown, 1821.

Lay, William, and Cyrus M. Hussey. *A Narrative of the Mutiny, on board the Ship Globe of Nantucket, in the Pacific Ocean, Jan. 1824, and the Journal of a Residence of Two Years on the Mulgrave Islands.* New London: 1828.

Lutke, Fedor Petrovich. *Voyage autour du Monde, 1826–1829.* New York: Da Capo Press, 1971.

Lyman, Horace S. "Recollections of Horace Holden." *Quarterly of the Oregon Historical Society* 3 (1902), pp. 164–217.

Marche, Antoine-Alfred. *The Mariana Islands (Rapport General sur un Mission aux isles Mariannes),* trans. Sylvia E. Cheng. Mangilao, Guam: University of Guam, Micronesian Area Research Center, 1982.

Martin, Kenneth R, ed. *"Naked and a Prisioner": Captain C.*

Barnard's Narrative of Shipwreck in Palau, 1832–1833. Sharon, MA: Kendall Whaling Museum, 1980.

Moore, S. G. "Report of the First Voyage of the Missionary Packet Morning Star." *Nautical Magazine* 27 (1858), pp. 449–457, 529–536.

Morrell, Benjamin. *A Narrative of Four Voyages to the South Sea, North and South Pacific Ocean, Chinese Sea, Ethiopic and Southern Atlantic Ocean, Indian and Antarctic Ocean, from the Year 1822 to 1831.* New York: Harper, 1832.

Moss, Frederick J. *Through Atolls and Islands in the Great South Sea.* London: Sampson Low, 1889.

Mueller, Wilhelm. *Yap.* New York: Garland, 1979.

O'Connell, James F. *A Residence of Eleven Years in New Holland and the Caroline Islands,* ed. Saul H. Riesenberg. Pacific History Series, 4. Honolulu: University Press of Hawaii, 1972.

Olive y Garcia, F. *The Mariana Islands: Random Notes Concerning Them,* trans. Marjorie G. Driver. Mangilao, Guam: University of Guam, Micronesian Area Research Center, 1984.

Paullin, Charles Oscar. *American Voyages to the Orient 1690–1865: An Account of Merchant and Naval Activities in China, Japan, and Various Pacific Islands.* Annapolis: United States Naval Institute, 1971.

Le Perouse, Jean Francois Galaup de. *A Voyage Round the World in the Years 1785, 1786, 1787, 1788.* London: 1798.

Petit-Skinner, Solange. *The Nauruans.* San Francisco: MacDuff Press, 1981.

Phelan, Nancy. *Atoll Holiday.* Sydney: Angus & Robertson, 1958.

Pigafetta, Antonio. *Magellan's Voyage: A Narrative Account of the First Circumnavigation* trans. and ed. R. A. Skelton. New Haven, CT: Yale University Press, 1969.

Price, Willard. *Japan's Islands of Mystery.* New York: John Day, 1944.

Quiros, Pedro Fernandez de. *The Voyages of Pedro Fernandez de Quiros 1595–1606,* trans. and ed. Clements Markham. Hakluyt Society Series 2, 14 and 15. London: Hakluyt Society, 1904.

Robertson, Russell. ''The Caroline Islands.'' *Transactions of the Asiatic Society of Japan* 5 (1877), pp. 41–63.

Rochon, A. M. de. *Crozet's Voyage to Tasmania, New Zealand, the Ladrone Islands, and the Philippines in the Years 1771–1772,* trans. H. Ling Roth. London: 1891.

Rogers, Woodes. *A Cruising Voyage Round the World, First to the South Seas, Thence to the East Indies and Homeward by the Cape of Good Hope.* Amsterdam/New York: Israel/Da Capo, 1969.

Sabatier, Ernest. *Astride the Equator: An Account of the Gilbert Islands,* trans. Ursala Nixon. Melbourne: Oxford University Press, 1977.

Sanz, Manuel. *Description of the Mariana Islands, 1827.* MARC Educational Series, 10. Mangilao, Guam: University of Guam, Micronesian Area Research Center, 1991.

Schroeder, Seaton. *A Half Century of Naval Service.* New York: Appleton, 1922.

Segal, Harvey Gordon. *Kosrae: The Sleeping Awakens.* Kosrae: Kosrae Tourist Division, nd.

Seymour, Edward H. *My Naval Career and Travels.* London: Smith, Elder, 1911.

Stanley, Henry E.J.S. *The First Voyage Round the World by Magellan: Translated from the Accounts of Pigafetta and other Contemporary Writers.* Hakluyt Society Series 1, 52. London: Hakluyt Society, 1874.

Tetens, Alfred. *Among the Savages of the South Seas: Memoirs of Micronesia, 1862–1868 by Captain Alfred Tetens,* trans. Florence Mann Spoehr. Stanford: Stanford University Press, 1958.

Viviani, Nancy. *Nauru: Phosphate and Political Progress.* Honolulu: University of Hawaii Press, 1970.

Ward, R. Gerard, ed. *American Activities in the Central Pacific 1790–1870: A History, Geography and Ethnography Pertaining to American Involvement and Americans in the Pacific, Taken from Contemporary Newspapers, etc.* Ridgewood, NJ: Gregg Press, 1966–1967.

Whincup, T. *Nareau's Nation: A Portrait of the Gilbert Islands.* London: Stacey International, 1979.

Whipple, A.B.C. *Yankee Whalers of the South Seas.* Garden City: Doubleday, 1954.

Whitmee, S. J. *A Missionary Cruise in the South Pacific . . . in the Missionary Barque "John Williams," during 1870.* Sydney, Australia: Joseph Cook, 1871.

Wilkes, Charles. *Narrative of the United States Exploring Expedition During the Years 1838, 1839, 1840, 1841, 1842.* Philadelphia: Lea & Blanchard, 1845.

Wilson, James. *A Missionary Voyage to the Southern Pacific Ocean Performed in the Years 1796, 1797, 1798, in the Ship Duff.* London: T. Chapman, 1799.

Wilson, John. *The Cruise of the Gipsy, the Journal of John Wilson, Surgeon on a Whaling Voyage to the Pacific Ocean 1839–43,* ed. Honore Forster. Fairfield, WA: Ye Galleon Press, 1991.

Wright, Ione S., ed. *Voyages of Alvara de Saavedra ceron, 1527–1529.* University of Florida Hispanic-American Studies, 11. Coral Gables, FL: University of Miami Press, 1951.

EDUCATION

Aguon, Katherine. "The Guam Dilemma: The Need for a Pacific Island Education Perspective." *Amerasia* 6, 2 (1979), pp. 77–90.

Ballendorf, Dirk A. "Educational Development in Micronesia, 1945–1968." *Asian Culture Quarterly* 12, 4 (1984), pp. 51–56.

Colletta, Nat J. *American Schools for the Natives of Ponape: A Study of Education and Culture Change in Micronesia.* Honolulu: University of Hawaii Press, 1980.

Hezel, Francis X. "In Search of a Home: Colonial Education in Micronesia." *In Culture Learning: Concepts, Applications, and Research,* ed. Richard W. Brislin. Honolulu: East-West Center, 1977.

————. "Schools in Micronesia Prior to American Administration." *Pacific Studies* 8, 1 (1984), pp. 95–109.

Nevin, David. *The American Touch in Micronesia.* New York: W. W. Norton, 1977.

Shuster, Donald R. "Schooling in Micronesia during Japanese Mandate Rule." *Educational Perspectives* 18, 2 (1979), pp. 20–26.

Thompson, Laura M. *Guam and its People: A Study of Cultural Change and Colonial Education.* Princeton: Princeton University Press, 1947.

HISTORY

Alden, John E. "A Press in Paradise: The Beginnings of Printing in Micronesia." *The Papers of the Bibliographical Society of America* 38 (1944), pp. 269–283.

Amery, L. S. *The German Colonial Claim*. London: W. & R. Chambers, Ltd., 1939.

Ashby, Gene. *Ponape: An Island Argosy*. Eugene, OR: Rainy Day Press, 1983.

———, ed. *Never and Always: Micronesian Stories of the Origins of Islands, Landmarks, and Customs*. Eugene, OR: Rainy Day Press, 1983.

Ballendorf, Dirk A. "American Administration in the Trust Territory of the Pacific Islands, 1944–1968." *Asian Culture Quarterly* 12, 1 (1984), pp. 1–10.

———, and William L. Wuerch. "Captain Samuel J. Masters, US Consul to Guam, 1854–1856: Harbinger of American Pacific Expansion." *Diplomacy & Statecraft* 2, 3 (1991), pp. 306–326.

Beaglehole, J. C. *The Exploration of the Pacific*. Stanford, CA: Stanford University Press, 1966.

Beardsley, Charles, *Guam: Past and Present*. Tokyo: Charles E. Tuttle Co., 1964.

Beers, Henry P. *American Naval Occupation and Government of Guam, 1898–1902*. Administrative Reference Report, 6. Washington, DC: Navy Department, 1944.

Bennett, J. A. "Immigration, 'Blackbirding,' Labour Recruiting?" *Journal of Pacific History* 11 (1976) pp. 3–27.

Bernat, Luelen. *The Book of Leulen*, trans. and eds. John L. Fischer, Saul H. Risenberg, and Marjorie G. Whiting. Pacific History Series, 8. Honolulu: University of Hawaii Press, 1977.

Buck, Peter H. *Explorers of the Pacific*. Special Publications, 43. Honolulu: Bishop Museum, 1953.

Carano, Paul, and Pedro Sanchez. *A Complete History of Guam.* Rutland, VT and Tokyo: Charles E, Tuttle, 1964.

Chatterton, E. Keble. *Whalers and Whaling.* London: T. Fisher Unwin, Ltd., 1925.

Cholmondeley, Lionel Berners. *The History of the Bonin Islands from the Year 1827 to the Year 1876 and of Nathaniel Savory, One of the Original Settlers to Which is Added a Short Supplement Dealing with the Islands after Their Occupation by the Japanese.* London: Constable, 1915.

Christmann, Helmut, Peter Hempstall, and Dirk A. Ballendorf. *The Caroline Islands in German Times: A Case Study in Colonial History.* Bremen: University of Bremen, 1991.

Clune, Frank. *Captain Bully Hayes: Blackbirder and Bigamist.* Sydney: Angus and Robertson, 1970.

Clyde, P. *Japan's Pacific Mandate.* New York: Macmillan Co., 1935.

Corte y Ruano Calderon, Felipe de la. "A History of the Marianas Islands from the Time of the Arrival of the Spaniards to the 5th of May 1870, with Continuation by Padre Jose Palomo." Typescript. University of Guam, Micronesian Area Research Center.

Dana, Julian. *Gods Who Die: The Story of Samoa's Greatest Adventurer.* New York: Macmillan, 1935.

Del Valle, Teresa. *The Importance of the Mariana Islands to Spain at the Beginning of the Nineteenth Century.* MARC Educational Series, 11. Mangilao, Guam: University of Guam, Micronesian Area Research Center, 1991.

Delgadillo, Yolanda et al. *Spanish Forts of Guam.* Mangilao, Guam: University of Guam, Micronesian Area Research Center, 1979.

Dodge, Ernest S. *Beyond the Capes: Pacific Exploration from Captain Cook to the Challenger (1776–1877)*. Boston: Little, Brown, 1971.

———. *New England and the South Seas*. Cambridge, MA: Harvard University Press, 1965.

Driver, Marjorie G. "Fray Juan Probre de Zamora and his Account of the Mariana Islands." *Journal of Pacific History* 18 (1983) pp. 198–216.

Dunbablin, Thomas. *Slavers of the South Seas*. Sydney, Australia: Angus and Robertson, 1935.

Dunmore, John. *French Explorers in the Pacific. Vol. 2. The Nineteenth Century*. Oxford: Clarendon Press, 1969.

Ellis, Albert. *Ocean Island and Nauru: Their Story*. Sydney: Angus and Robertson, 1935.

Fahey, James J. *Pacific War Diary*. New York: Avon Books, 1963.

Farrell, Andrew. *John Cameron's Odyssey*. New York: Macmillan, 1928.

Farrell, Don A. *The Pictorial History of Guam: Liberation–1944*. Tamuning, Guam: Micronesian Productions, 1984.

———. *The Pictorial History of Guam: The Americanizatione 1898–1918*. Tamuning, Guam: Micronesian Productions, 1986.

———. *The Pictorial History of Guam: The Sacrifice 1919–1943*. San Jose, Tinian, Commonwealth of the Northern Mariana Islands: Micronesian Productions, 1991.

Firth, Stewart. "German Labour Policy on Nauru and Angaur, 1906–1914." *Journal of Pacific History* 13, 1–2 (1978), pp. 36–52.

Fischer, John L, and Saul H. Riesenberg, and Marjorie G. Whiting. *Annotations to the Book of Luelen.* Pacific History Series, 9. Honolulu: University of Hawaii Press, 1977.

Fritz, Georg. *The Chamorros: A History and Ethnography of the Mariana Islands,* trans. E. Craddock. Mangilao, Guam: University of Guam, Micronesian Area Research Center, 1984.

Fritz, Georg. *The Chamorro: A History and Ethnography of the Marianas,* trans. Elfriede Craddock. Saipan: Division of Historic Preservation, 1989.

Garcia, Francisco. *The Life and Martyrdom of the Venerable Father Diego Luis de Sanvitores,* trans. Margaret Higgens. Agana, Guam: Nieves M. Flores Memorial Library, 1985.

Le Gobien, Charles. *Historie des Isles Marianes, nouvellement converties a la Religion Chrestienne; et du martyr des premiers Apostres qui y ont presche la Foy.* Paris: Pepie, 1700.

Grattan, C. Hartley. *The Southwest Pacific to 1900: A Modern History—Australia, New Zealand, The Islands, Antarctica.* Ann Arbor: University of Michigan Press, 1963.

Hanlon, David L. "God Versus Gods: First Years of the Micronesian Mission on Ponape, 1852–1859." *Journal of Pacific History* 19 (1984), pp 41–59.

Hanlon, David. *Upon a Stone Altar: A History of the Island of Pohnpei to 1890.* Pacific Islands Monograph Series, 5. Honolulu: University of Hawaii Press, 1988.

Haynes, Douglas E., and William L. Wuerch. *Historical Survey of the Spanish Mission Sites on Guam.* Guam: University of Guam, Micronesian Area Research Center, 1990.

Hempenstall, P. J. *Pacific Islanders under German Rule: A Study in the Meaning of Colonial Resistance.* Canberrra, Australia: Australian National University Press, 1978.

Hezel, Francis X. "The Beginnings of Foreign Contact with Truk." *Journal of Pacific History* 8 (1973), pp. 51–73.

———. "Catholic Missions in the Caroline and Marshall Islands: A Survey of Historical Materials." *Journal of Pacific History* 5 (1970), pp. 213–227.

———. *The First Taint of Civilization: A History of the Caroline and Marshall Islands in Pre-Colonial Days, 1521–1885.* Pacific Islands Monograph Series, 1. Honolulu: University of Hawaii Press, 1983.

———. "From Conversion to Conquest: The Early Spanish Mission in the Marianas." *Journal of Pacific History* 17, 3 (1982), pp. 115–137.

———. "The Role of the Beachcomber in the Carolines." *In the Changing Pacific,* ed. Neil Gunson. Melbourne: Oxford University Press, 1978, pp. 261–272.

———. "Schools in Micronesia Prior to American Administration." *Pacific Studies* 8, 1 (1984), pp. 95–109.

———. "A Yankee Trader in Yap: Crayton Philo Holcomb." *Journal of Pacific History* 10 (1975), pp. 3–19.

———, and Mark L. Berg, eds. *Micronesia, Winds of Change: A Book of Readings on Micronesian History.* Saipan: Trust Territory of the Pacific Islands, 1979.

———, and Maria Teresa del Valle. "Early European Contact with the Western Carolines." *Journal of Pacific History* 7 (1972), pp. 26–44.

A History of Palau. Palau Community Action Agency. Guam: Navy Printing, 1977–1978.

Howe, K. R. *Where the Waves Fall: A New South Sea Islands History from the First Settlement to Colonial Rule.* Pacific Islands Monograph Series, 2. Honolulu: University of Hawaii Press, 1984.

Hoyt, Edwin P. *The Mutiny on the "Globe."* New York: Random House, 1975.

Hunt, Cornelius E. *The Shenandoah; or the Last Confederate Cruiser.* New York: G. W. Carlton, 1867.

Ibanez, A. *Chronicle of the Mariana Islands,* trans. Marjorie G. Driver. Mangilao, Guam: University of Guam, Micronesian Area Research Center, 1974.

Ibanez del Carmen, Aniceto, and Francisco Resano, et al. *Chronicle of the Mariana Islands,* trans. Marjorie D. Driver. Mangilao, Guam: University of Guam, Micronesia Area Research Center, 1976.

Ibanez y Garcia, Luis de. *History of the Mariana, Caroline, and Palau Islands.* MARC Educational Series, 12. Mangilao, Guam: University of Guam, Micronesian Area Research Center, 1992.

Johnston, Emilie, ed. *Sanvitores: His Life, Times and Martyrdom.* Mangilao, Guam: University of Guam, Micronesian Area Research Center, 1977.

Klingman, Lawrence, and Gerald Green. *His Majesty O'Keefe.* New York: Scribner, 1950.

Lessa, William A. "Drake in the Marianas?" *Micronesica* 10 (1974), pp. 7–11.

———. *Drake's Island of Thieves: Ethnological Sleuthing.* Honolulu: University of Hawaii Press, 1975.

———. "The Portuguese Discovery of the Isles of Sequeira." *Micronesica* 11 (1975), pp. 35–70.

Logan, Robert W. *The Work of God in Micronesia, 1852–1883.* Boston: ABCFM, 1884.

Macdonald, Barrie. *Cinderellas of the Empire: Towards a History of Kiribati and Tuvalu.* Canberra, Australia: Australian National University Press, 1982.

————. "The Separation of the Gilbert and Ellice Islands." *Journal of Pacific History* 10, 4 (1975), pp. 84–88.

Maga, Timothy P. *Defending Paradise: The United States and Guam, 1898–1950.* New York: Garland, 1988.

Margalith, Aaron. *The International Mandates.* Baltimore: Johns Hopkins Press, 1930.

Maude, H. E. *Of Islands and Men: Studies in Pacific History.* Melbourne: Oxford University Press, 1968.

Maude, Henry E. *The Evolution of Gilbertese Boti: An Ethnohistorical Interpretation.* Suva, Fiji: University of the South Pacific, Institute of Pacific Studies, 1977.

May, Dean. "Captain O'Keefe—the King of Yap." *Argosy,* May (1969), pp. 36–39; 84–87.

Morrell, W. P. *Britain in the Pacific Ocean.* Oxford: Clarendon, 1960.

Moses, John A. and Paul M. Kennedy, eds. *Germany in the Pacific and Far East, 1870–1914.* St. Lucia: University of Queensland Press, 1977.

Nozikov, Nikolai N. *Russian Voyages Round the World.* London: Hutchinson, 1946.

Nufer, Harold F. *Micronesia under American Rule: An Evaluation of the Strategic Trusteeship, 1947–1977.* Hicksville, NY: Exposition Press, 1978.

Oliver, Douglas L. *The Pacific Islands.* New York: Doubleday, 1975.

Palomo, Jose R. *Recollections of Olden Days.* MARC Educational Series, 13. Mangilao, Guam: University of Guam, Micronesian Area Research Center, 1992.

Parmentier, Richard J. *The Sacred Remains: Myth, History, and Polity in Belau.* Chicago: University of Chicago Press, 1987.

Paullin, Charles Oscar. *American Voyages to the Orient 1690–1865: An Account of Merchant and Naval Activities in China, Japan, and Various Pacific Islands.* Annapolis, MD: United States Naval Institute, 1971.

Pauwels, Peter C. *The Japanese Mandate Islands.* Bandoeng, Indonesia: Van Dorp, 1936.

Peacock, Daniel J. *Lee Boo of Belau: A Prince in London.* South Seas Books, 1. Honolulu: University of Hawaii Press, 1987.

Peattie, Mark R. *Nanyo: The Rise and Fall of the Japanese in Micronesia, 1885–1945.* Pacific Islands Monograph Series, 4. Honolulu: University of Hawaii Press, 1988.

Pomeroy, Earl S. *Pacific Outpost: American Strategy in Guam and Micronesia.* Stanford, CA: Stanford University Press, 1951.

Poyer, Linette. "The Ngatik Massacre: Documentary and Oral Traditional Accounts." *Journal of Pacific History* 20, 1 (1985), pp. 4–22.

Purcell, David C., Jr. "The Economics of Exploitation: The Japanese in the Mariana, Caroline, and Marshall Islands." *Journal of Pacific History* 11, 3 (1976), pp. 189–211.

Ralston, Caroline. *Grass Huts and Warehouses: Pacific Beach Communities of the 19th Century.* Honolulu: University of Hawaii Press, 1978.

Reed, Erik K. *Archaeology and History of Guam.* Washington, DC: National Park Service, 1952.

Richard, Dorothy. *History of U.S. Naval Administration of the Trust Territory of the Pacific Islands.* Washington, DC: Office of Naval Operations, 1957.

Riesenberg, Saul H. "The Tattooed Irishman." *The Smithsonian Journal of History* 3 (1968), pp. 1–18.

Rogers, Robert F. *Guam's Search for Commonwealth.* MARC Educational Series, 7. Mangilao, Guam: University of Guam, Micronesian Area Research Center, 1984.

Safford, William Edwin. *The Useful Plants of Guam, with an Introductory Account of the Physical Features and Natural History of the Island, of the Character and History of its People, and of their Agriculture.* Washington, DC: National Museum, 1905.

Sanchez, Pedro C. *Guahan Guam: The History of our Island.* Agana, Guam: Sanchez Publishing, 1990.

Scarr, Deryck. *Fragments of Empire: A History of the Western Pacific High Commission 1877–1914.* Canberra, Australia: Australian National University Press, 1967.

———. *More Pacific Islands Portraits.* Canberra, Australia: Australian National University Press, 1978.

Schurz, William L. *The Manila Galleon.* New York: E. P. Dutton, 1939.

Sharp, Andrew. *Adventurous Aramada: The Story of Legazpi's Expedition.* Christchurch, New Zealand: Whitcombe and Tombs, 1961.

———. *The Discovery of the Pacific Islands.* Oxford: Clarendon, 1960.

Shuster, Donald R. "Schooling in Micronesia during Japanese Mandate Rule." *Educational Perspectives* 18, 2 (1979), pp. 20–26.

———. "State Shinto in Micronesia during Japanese Rule, 1914–1945." *Pacific Studies* 5, 2 (1992), pp. 20–43.

Spate, O.H.K. *The Spanish Lake. The Pacific since Magellan,* vol. 1. Canberra, Australia: Australian National University Press, 1979.

Spoehr, Florence Mann. *White Falcon: The House of Godeffroy and Its Commercial and Scientific Role in the Pacific.* Palo Alto, CA: Pacific Books, 1963.

Stackpole, Edouard A. *The Sea-Hunters: The New England Whalemen During the Two Centuries: 1635–1835.* Philadelphia: Lippincott, 1953.

Stevens, Russell L. *Guam, USA: Birth of a Territory.* Honolulu: Tongg Publishing, 1953.

Sullivan, Julius O.F.M. Cap. *The Phoenix Rises: A Mission History of Guam.* New York: Seraphic Mass Association, 1957.

Talu, Alaima, et al. *Kiribati: Aspects of History.* Tarawa, Kiribati: Ministry of Education, Training and Culture, 1979.

Thompson, Laura M. *Guam and its People: A Study of Cultural Change and Colonial Education.* Princeton, NJ: Princeton University Press, 1947.

Townsend, Mary. *The Rise and Fall of Germany's Colonial Empire.* New York: Macmillan, 1950.

Trumbull, Robert. *Paradise in Trust: A Report on Americans in Micronesia, 1946–1958.* New York: W. Sloane Associates, 1959.

Twenty-eight Years in the Guam Jungle: Sergeant Yokoi Home from World War II. Tokyo: Japan Publications, Inc., 1972.

Walter, Richard. *Anson's Voyage Round the World.* London: Martin Hopkinson, 1928.

Ward, R. Gerard, ed. *American Activities in the Central Pacific 1790–1870: A History, Geography and Ethnography Pertaining to American Involvement and Americans in the*

Pacific, Taken from Contemporary Newspapers, etc. Ridgewood, NJ: Gregg Press, 1966–1967.

Whipple, A.B.C. *Yankee Whalers of the South Seas.* Garden City:
Doubleday, 1954.

Wiltgen, Ralph M. *The Founding of the Roman Catholic Church
in Oceania 1825 to 1850.* Canberra, Australia: Australian
National University Press, 1979.

Wright, Quincy. *Mandates under the League of Nations.* Chicago:
University of Chicago Press, 1930.

Yanaihara, Tadao. *Pacific Islands under Japanese Mandate.*
London: Oxford University Press, 1940.

HISTORY—WORLD WAR II

Apple, Richard A. *Guam: Two Invasions and Three Military
Occupations.* Mangilao, Guam: University of Guam, Micronesian Area Research Center, 1980.

Ellis, Earl Hancock. "Operation Plan 712: Advanced Base Opera-
tions in Micronesia." 1921. U.S. Marine Corps, History and
Museums Division and University of Guam, Micronesian
Area Research Center.

Gailey, Harry A. *Howlin' Mad vs the Army: Conflict in Command, Saipan 1944.* Novato, CA: Presidio Press, 1986.

———. *Peleliu, 1944.* Annapolis, MD: Nautical & Aviation
Publishing Company, 1983.

Guam: Operations of the 77th Division (21 July–10 August 1944).
Washington, DC: War Department, Historical Division,
1946.

Hoffman, Carl W. *Saipan: The Beginning of the End.* Washington, DC: U.S. Marine Corps, Historical Division, 1950.

————. *The Seizure of Tinian.* Washington, DC: U.S. Marine Corps, Historical Division, 1951.

Hoyt, Edwin P. *Storm over the Gilberts: War in the Central Pacific, 1943.* New York: Van Nostrand Reinhold Co., 1978.

————. *To the Marianas: War in the Central Pacific.* New York: Avon Books, 1983.

Lodge, C. R. *The Recapture of Guam.* Washington, DC: U.S. Government Printing Office, 1954.

Morison, Samuel Eliot. *History of the U.S. Naval Operations in World War II, Vol. VII, Aleutians, Gilberts and Marshalls.* Boston: Little, Brown, 1952.

Richardson, W. *The Epic of Tarawa.* London: Odhams Press Ltd., nd.

Ross, Bill D. *Peleliu, Tragic Triumph: The Untold Story of the Pacific War's Forgotten Battle.* New York: Random House, 1991.

Shaw, Henry I., Jr. *Tarawa, a Legend is Born.* New York: Ballantine Books, Inc., 1968.

Sherrod, Robert. *Tarawa: The Story of a Battle.* New York: Duell, Sloan & Pearce, 1944.

Spoehr, Alexander. *Saipan: The Ethnology of a War-Devastated Island.* Fieldiana: Anthropology, 39. Chicago: Natural History Museum, 1954.

Thomas, Gordon; Witts, Max Morgan. *Enola Gay.* New York: Pocket Books, 1977.

LANGUAGE

Abo, Takaji. *Marshallese-English Dictionary.* Honolulu: University Press of Hawaii, 1976.

Clark, Raymond C., and Stephen Trussel. *Kiribati (Gilbertese): Teacher's Handbook.* Washington, DC: Peace Corps, 1979.

Goodenough, Ward H., and Hiroshi Sugita. *Trukese-English Dictionary.* Philadelphia: American Philosophical Society, 1980.

Jensen, John T. *Yapese Reference Grammar.* Honolulu: University of Hawaii Press, 1977.

————. *Yapese-English Dictionary.* Honolulu: University of Hawaii Press, 1977.

Josephs, Lewis S. *Palauan Reference Grammar.* Honolulu: University of Hawaii Press, 1975.

Lee, Kee-dong. *Kusaiean Reference Grammar.* Honolulu: University of Hawaii Press, 1975.

————. *Kusaiean-English Dictionary.* Honolulu: University of Hawaii Press, 1976.

McManus, Edwin G. *Palauan-English Dictionary.* Honolulu: University of Hawaii Press, 1977.

Rehg, Kenneth L. *Ponapean-English Dictionary.* Honolulu: University of Hawaii Press, 1979.

————. *Ponapean Reference Grammar.* Honolulu: University of Hawaii Press, 1981.

Topping, Donald M. *Chamorro-English Dictionary.* Honolulu: University of Hawaii Press, 1975.

————, Pedro M. Ogo. *Spoken Chamorro, with Grammatical Notes and Glossary.* Honolulu: University of Hawaii Press, 1980.

POLITICS AND GOVERNMENT

Amery, L. S. *The German Colonial Claim.* London: W. & R. Chambers, Ltd., 1939.

Ballendorf, Dirk A. "American Administration in the Trust Territory of the Pacific Islands, 1944–1968." *Asian Culture Quarterly* 12, 1 (1984), pp. 1–10.

Beers, Henry P. *American Naval Occupation and Government of Guam, 1898–1902.* Administrative Reference Report, 6. Washington, DC: Navy Department, 1944.

De Smith, Stanley A. *Microstates and Micronesia: Problems of America's Pacific Islands and Other Minute Territories.* New York: New York University Press, 1970.

Force, Roland W., ed. *Induced Political Change in the Pacific: A Symposium.* Honolulu: Bishop Museum, 1965.

Gale, R. W. *The Americanization of Micronesia: A Study of the Consolodation of U.S. Rule in the Pacific.* Washington, DC: University Press of America, 1979.

Geographic, Military, and Political Description of the Island of Guam, trans. Francisco Ramon de Villalobos. Felicia Plaza. MARC Working Papers, 8. Mangilao, Guam: University of Guam, Micronesian Area Research Center, 1969.

Gracia y Parejo, Rafael. *Considerations on the Rights of Spain over the Caroline Islands,* ed. Patricia Bieber. Miscellaneous Working Papers, 1. Honolulu: University of Hawaii, Pacific Islands Program, 1973.

Heine, Carl. *Micronesia at the Crossroads. A Reappraisal of the Micronesian Political Dilemma.* Honolulu: University of Hawaii Press, 1974.

Hughes, Daniel T., and Sherwood G. Lingenfelter, eds. *Political Development in Micronesia.* Columbus: Ohio State University Press, 1974.

Kluge, P. F. *The Edge of Paradise: America in Micronesia.* New York: Random House, 1991.

Lingenfelter, Sherwood G. *Yap: Political Leadership and Culture Change in an Island Society.* Honolulu: University of Hawaii Press, 1975.

Macdonald, Barrie. "Constitutional Development in the Gilbert and Ellice Islands Colony." *Journal of Pacific History* 5 (1970), pp. 139–145.

————. "The Separation of the Gilbert and Ellice Islands." *Journal of Pacific History* 10, 4 (1975), pp. 84–88.

McHenry, D. F. *Micronesia: Trust Betrayed. Altruism vs. Self-Interest in American Foreign Policy.* New York: Carnegie Endowment for International Peace, 1975.

Micronesian Politics. Politics of the Pacific Islands, 3. Suva, Fiji: Institute of Pacific Studies, University of the South Pacific, 1988.

Nufer, Harold F. *Micronesia under American Rule: An Evaluation of the Strategic Trusteeship, 1947–1977.* Hicksville, NY: Exposition Press, 1978.

Petersen, Glenn T. *One Man Cannot Rule a Thousand: Fission in a Ponapean Chiefdom.* Ann Arbor, MI: University of Michigan Press, 1982.

Politics in Kiribati. Tarawa and Suva: Kiribati Extension Centre and the Institute of Pacific Studies, University of the South Pacific, 1980.

Purcell, David C., Jr. "The Economics of Exploitation: The Japanese in the Mariana, Caroline, and Marshall Islands." *Journal of Pacific History* 11, 3 (1976), pp. 189–211.

Rogers, Robert F. *Guam's Commonwealth Effort, 1987–1988.* MARC Educational Series, 8. Mangilao, Guam: University of Guam, Micronesian Area Research Center, 1987.

————. *Guam's Search for Commonwealth.* MARC Educational Series, 7. Mangilao, Guam: University of Guam, Micronesian Area Research Center, 1984.

Souder-Jaffery, Laura, and Robert A. Underwood, eds. *Chamorro Self-Determination: The Right of a People.* MARC Education Series, 7. Mangilao, Guam: University of Guam, Micronesian Area Research Center, 1987.

Trumbull, Robert. *Paradise in Trust: A Report on Americans in Micronesia, 1946–1958.* New York: W. Sloane Associates, 1959.

————. *Tin Roofs and Palm Trees: A Report on the New South Seas.* Seattle and London: University of Washington Press, 1977.

Viviani, Nancy. *Nauru: Phosphate and Political Progress.* Honolulu: University of Hawaii Press, 1970.

Wenkam, Robert, and Byron Baker. *Micronesia—The Breadfruit Revolution.* Honolulu: East-West Center, 1971.

Wright, Quincy. *Mandates under the League of Nations.* Chicago: University of Chicago Press, 1930.

Yanaihara, Tadao. *Pacific Islands under Japanese Mandate.* London: Oxford University Press, 1940.

REFERENCE

Bendure, Glenda, and Ned Friary. *Micronesia: A Travel Survival Kit.* Berkeley, CA: Lonely Planet Publications, 1988.

Bryan, E. H., Jr. *Guide to Place names in the Trust Territory of the Pacific Islands (the Marshall, Caroline, and Mariana Islands).* Honolulu: Bishop Museum, 1971.

Craig, Robert D., and Frank P. King. *Historical Dictionary of Oceania.* Westport, CT: Greenwood Press, 1981.

Douglas, Norman and Ngaire Douglas, eds. *Pacific Islands Yearbook.* North Ryde, New South Wales: Angus & Robertson, 1989.

Driver, Marjorie G. *Guam: A Nomenclature Chronology.* MARC Educational Series, 5. Mangilao, Guam: University of Guam, Micronesian Area Research Center, 1985.

Hezel, Francis. *Foreign Ships in Micronesia.* Saipan: Historic Preservation Office, 1979.

Karolle, Bruce. *Atlas of Micronesia.* Agana, Guam: Guam Publications, Inc., 1987.

Levesque, Rodrique. *Ships Through Micronesia: A Chronological Listing of Significant Ships That Passed Through Micronesian Waters from Magellan's Time to the Present, 1521–1991.* Gatineau, Quebec, Canada: Levesque Publications, 1991.

Lingenfelter, Richard E. *Presses of the Pacific Islands, 1817–1867.* Los Angeles: Plantin Press, 1967.

Motteler, Lee S. *Pacific Island Names.* Honolulu: Bishop Museum, 1986.

Ridgell, Reilly. *Pacific Nations and Territories: The Islands of Micronesia, Melanesia, and Polynesia.* Honolulu: Base Press, Inc., 1988.

Stanley, David. *Micronesia Handbook: Guide to the Caroline, Gilbert, Mariana, and Marshall Islands.* Chico, CA: Moon Publications, 1989.

Ward, R. Gerard, ed. *American Activities in the Central Pacific 1790–1870: A History, Geography and Ethnography Pertaining to American Involvement and Americans in the Pacific, Taken from Contemporary Newspapers, etc.* Ridgewood, NJ: Gregg Press, 1966–1967.

RELIGION

Bliss, Theodora Crosby. *Micronesia: Fifty Years in the Island World.* Boston: ABCFM, 1906.

Boutilier, James A, ed. *Mission, Church, and Sect in Oceania.* Ann Arbor, MI: University of Michigan Press, 1978.

Crawford, David, and Leona Crawford. *Missionary Adventures in the South Pacific.* Rutland, VT and Tokyo: Charles E. Tuttle, 1967.

Garcia, Francisco. *The Life and Martyrdom of the Venerable Father Diego Luis de San Vitores,* trans. Margaret Higgens. Agana, Guam: Nieves M. Flores Memorial Library, 1985.

Le Gobien, Charles. *Historie des Isles Marianes, nouvellement converties a la Religion Chrestienne; et du martyr des premiers Apostres qui y ont presche la Foy.* Paris: Pepie, 1700.

Gulick, Luther H. "Lectures on Micronesia." *52nd Annual Report of the Hawaiian Historical Society.* Honolulu: Hawaiian Historical Society, 1943.

Hanlon, David L. "God Versus Gods: First Years of the Micronesian Mission on Ponape, 1852–1859." *Journal of Pacific History* 19 (1984), pp. 41–59.

Hezel, Francis X. "Catholic Missions in the Caroline and Marshall Islands: A Survey of Historical Materials." *Journal of Pacific History* 5 (1970), pp. 213–227.

———. "From Conversion to Conquest: The Early Spanish Mission in the Marianas." *Journal of Pacific History* 17, 3 (1982), pp. 115–137.

Johnstone, Emile, ed. *San Vitores: His Life, Times and Martyrdom.* Mangilao, Guam: University of Guam, Micronesian Area Research Center, 1977.

Logan, Mary. *Last Words and Work of Reverend Robert W. Logan.* Boston: ABCFM, 1888.

———. *The Work of God in Micronesia, 1852–1883.* Boston: ABCFM, 1884.

O'Brien, Ilma E. "Missionaries on Ponape: Induced Social and Political Change." *Australian National University Historical Journal* 8 (1971), pp. 53–64.

Shuster, Donald R. "State Shinto in Micronesia during Japanese Rule, 1914–1945." *Pacific Studies* 5, 2 (1982), pp. 20–43.

Sullivan, Julius O.F.M. Cap. *The Phoenix Rises: A Mission History of Guam.* New York: Seraphic Mass Association, 1957.

Whitmee, S. J. *A Missionary Cruise in the South Pacific . . . in the Missionary Barque "John Williams," during 1870.* Sydney: Joseph Cook, 1871.

Wilson, James. *A Missionary Voyage to the Southern Pacific Ocean Performed in the Years 1796, 1797, 1798, in the Ship "Duff."* London: T. Chapman, 1799.

Wiltgen, Ralph M. *The Founding of the Roman Catholic Church in Oceania 1825 to 1850.* Canberra, Australia: Australian National University Press, 1979.

Wright, Cliff. *Christ and Kiribati Culture.* Kiribati: Protestant Church, 1981.

SOCIETY

Alkire, William H. *Lamotrek Atoll and Inter-Island Socioeconomic Ties.* Illinois Studies in Anthropology, 5. Urbana, IL: University of Illinois Press, 1965.

Barnett, H. G. *Palauan Society: A Study in Contemporary Native Life in the Palau Islands.* Eugene, OR: University of Oregon Publications, 1949.

Bates, Marston and Donald Abbot. *Ifaluk: Portrait of a Coral Island.* London: Museum Press Ltd., 1959.

Fischer, John L. *The Eastern Carolines.* New Haven, CT: Human Relations Area Files Press, 1970.

Force, Roland W., ed. *Induced Political Change in the Pacific: A Symposium.* Honolulu: Bishop Museum, 1965.

Fritz, Georg. *The Chamorros: A History and Ethnography of the Mariana Islands,* trans. E. Craddock. Mangilao, Guam: University of Guam, Micronesian Area Research Center, 1984.

———. *The Chamorro: A History of Ethnography of the Marianas,* trans. Elfriede Craddock. Saipan: Division of Historic Preservation, 1989.

Gladwin, Thomas. *East is a Big Bird: Navigation and Logic on Puluwat Atoll.* Cambridge, MA: Harvard University Press, 1970.

———, and Seymour B. Sarason. *Truk: Man in Paradise.* Viking Fund Publications in Anthropology, 20. New York: Wenner-Gren Foundation for Anthropological Research, 1953.

Goodenough, Ward H. *Property, Kin, and Community on Truk.* Hamden, CT: Archon Books, 1978.

Hidikata, H. *Palauan Kinship.* Mangilao, Guam: University of Guam, Micronesian Area Research Center, 1973.

Joseph, Alice, and Veronica Murray. *Chamorros and Carolinians of Saipan.* Cambridge, MA: Harvard University Press, 1951.

Kiste, Robert C. *The Bikinians: A Study in Forced Migration.* Menlo Park, CA: Cummings Publishing Company, 1974.

Kubary, Johann Stanislaus. "Die Palau-Inseln in der Sudsee." *Journal des Museum Godeffroy* 1 (1873), pp. 177–238.

————. "Uber des Einheimische Geld auf der Insel Yap und auf den Palau Inseln." *In Ethnographische Beitrage zur Kenntnis des Karolinen Archipels.* Leiden: van der Hoek, 1889.

Lessa, William A. "An Evaluation of Early Descriptions of Carolinian Culture." *Ethnohistory* 9 (1962), pp. 313–403.

————. *Ulithi: A Micronesian Design for Living.* New York: Holt, Rinehart and Winston, 1966.

Lundsgaarde, Henry P. *Social Changes in the Southern Gilbert Islands: 1938–1964.* Eugene, OR: University of Oregon, nd.

Mason, Leonard, ed. *Kiribati: A Changing Atoll Culture.* Suva, Fiji: University of the South Pacific, Institute of Pacific Studies, 1985.

O'Brien, Ilma E. "Missionaries on Ponape: Induced Social and Political Change." *Australian National University Historical Journal* 8 (1971), pp. 53–64.

Parmentier, Richard J. *The Sacred Remains: Myth, History, and Polity in Belau.* Chicago: University of Chicago Press, 1987.

Riesenberg, Saul H. *The Native Polity of Ponape.* Smithsonian Contributions to Anthropology, 10. Washington, DC: Smithsonian Press, 1968.

Semper, K. *The Palau Islands in the Pacific,* trans. Mark L. Berg. Mangilao, Guam: University of Guam, Micronesian Area Research Center, 1982.

Spoehr, Alexander. *Majuro: A Village in the Marshall Islands.* Fieldiana: Anthropology, 39. Chicago: Natural History Museum, 1949.

ABOUT THE AUTHORS

WILLIAM L. WUERCH was born in the United States and educated in the public schools there and in Australia. He earned a bachelor's degree from Kent State University (1975), an M.A. in history from the University of Oregon (1979) and an MLS from the University of Hawaii (1981). He has worked in libraries and archives in the region since then, serving as Guam's Assistant Territorial Librarian and as associate professor of library science at Robert F. Kennedy Library, the main library at the University of Guam. He is currently manuscripts librarian at the University of Guam's Micronesian Area Research Center. Professor Wuerch has published many popular and scholarly articles and has coauthored two reference books, *Micronesia 1975–1987: A Social Science Bibliography* (Greenwood, 1989) and *Micronesian Folklore and Indigenous Religions: An Annotated Bibliography* (Greenwood, forthcoming).

DIRK ANTHONY BALLENDORF was born in Philadelphia, Pennsylvania, in 1939 and educated in the public schools there. In 1961 he graduated from the Pennsylvania State College at West Chester, and as a history teacher spent the following two years as a Peace Corps Volunteer in the Philippines. He received further education at Howard University and at Harvard. In Micronesia he has served as director of the Peace Corps in Palau and as associate director of Peace Corps/Micronesia at Saipan. In the late 1970s he was president of the Community College of Micronesia at Pohnpei in the Eastern Caroline Islands. He is professor of Micronesian studies at the University of Guam's Micronesian Area Research Center where he has been since 1979, serving as director there for five years. Dr. Ballendorf has also been a visiting professor, scholar, and lecturer at universities in Australia, New Zealand, Germany, the Soviet Union, and on the U.S. mainland. Locally, Professor Ballendorf has been editor of *Glimpses Magazine,* a regional quarterly published on Guam, and a historical features journalist on K-57 Radio.